W9-ADU-048

THE DARK TOWER

THE DARK TOWER

Nineteenth Century Narrative Poems

Compiled by

DAIRINE COFFEY

Acknowledgments

The illustrations in this book are from *1800 Woodcuts by Thomas Bewick and His School*, published by Dover Publications, Inc.

"The Sacrilege" by Thomas Hardy was reprinted with permission of The Macmillan Company from *Collected Poems* by Thomas Hardy.

International Standard Book Number 0-8486-0008-8

Library of Congress Catalog Number 78-74508

Reprinted 1979 by special arrangement
with Atheneum Publishers.

PRINTED IN THE UNITED STATES OF AMERICA

CONTENTS

CONTENTS

THE DARK TOWER

Lord Byron

THE PRISONER OF CHILLON

I

My hair is gray, but not with years,
Nor grew it white
In a single night,
As men's have grown from sudden fears;
My limbs are bowed, though not with toil,
But rusted with a vile repose,
For they have been a dungeon's spoil,
And mine has been the fate of those
To whom the goodly earth and air
Are banned, and barred—forbidden fare:
But this was for my father's faith
I suffered chains and courted death;
That father perished at the stake
For tenets he would not forsake;
And for the same his lineal race
In darkness found a dwelling-place;
We were seven—who now are one,
Six in youth, and one in age,
Finished as they had begun,
Proud of Persecution's rage;

One in fire, and two in field,
Their belief with blood have sealed,
Dying as their father died,
For the God their foes denied;
Three were in a dungeon cast,
Of whom this wreck is left the last.

II

There are seven pillars of Gothic mold,
In Chillon's dungeons deep and old,
There are seven columns, massy and gray,
Dim with a dull imprisoned ray,
A sunbeam which hath lost its way,
And through the crevice and the cleft
Of the thick wall is fallen and left;
Creeping o'er the floor so damp,
Like a marsh's meteor lamp:
And in each pillar there is a ring,
    And in each ring there is a chain;
That iron is a cankering thing,
    For in these limbs its teeth remain,
With marks that will not wear away,
Till I have done with this new day,
Which now is painful to these eyes,
Which have not seen the sun so rise
For years—I cannot count them o'er,
I lost their long and heavy score,
When my last brother drooped and died,
And I lay living by his side.

III

They chained us each to a column stone,
And we were three—yet, each alone;
We could not move a single pace,
We could not see each other's face,
But with that pale and livid light
That made us strangers in our sight:

And thus together—yet apart,
Fettered in hand, but joined in heart,
'Twas still some solace, in the dearth
Of the pure elements of earth,
To hearken to each other's speech,
And each turn comforter to each
With some new hope, or legend old,
Or song heroically bold;
But even these at length grew cold.
Our voices took a dreary tone,
An echo of the dungeon stone,
    A grating sound, not full and free,
    As they of yore were wont to be:
    It might be fancy, but to me
They never sounded like our own.

IV

I was the eldest of the three,
    And to uphold and cheer the rest
    I ought to do—and did my best—
And each did well in his degree.
    The youngest, whom my father loved,
Because our mother's brow was given
To him, with eyes as blue as heaven—
    For him my soul was sorely moved;
And truly might it be distressed
To see such bird in such a nest;
For he was beautiful as day—
    (When day was beautiful to me
    As to young eagles, being free)—
    A polar day, which will not see
A sunset till its summer's gone,
    Its sleepless summer of long light,
The snow-clad offspring of the sun;
    And thus he was as pure and bright,
And in his natural spirit gay,
With tears for nought but others' ills,

And then they flowed like mountain rills,
Unless he could assuage the woe
Which he abhorred to view below.

V

The other was as pure of mind,
But formed to combat with his kind;
Strong in his frame, and of a mood
Which 'gainst the world in war had stood,
And perished in the foremost rank
    With joy:—but not in chains to pine:
His spirit withered with their clank,
    I saw it silently decline—
    And so perchance in sooth did mine:
But yet I forced it on to cheer
Those relics of a home so dear.
He was a hunter of the hills
    Had followed there the deer and wolf;
    To him this dungeon was a gulf,
And fettered feet the worst of ills.

VI

    Lake Leman lies by Chillon's walls:
A thousand feet in depth below
Its massy waters meet and flow;
Thus much the fathom-line was sent
From Chillon's snow-white battlement,
    Which round about the wave enthralls:
A double dungeon wall and wave
Have made—and like a living grave
Below the surface of the lake
The dark vault lies wherein we lay:
We heard it ripple night and day;
    Sounding o'er our heads it knocked;

And I have felt the winter's spray
Wash through the bars when winds were high
And wanton in the happy sky;
    And then the very rock hath rocked,
    And I have felt it shake, unshocked,
Because I could have smiled to see
The death that would have set me free.

VII

I said my nearer brother pined,
I said his mighty heart declined,
He loathed and put away his food;
It was not that 'twas coarse and rude,
For we were used to hunter's fare,
And for the like had little care:
The milk drawn from the mountain goat
Was changed for water from the moat,
Our bread was such as captives' tears
Have moistened many a thousand years,
Since man first pent his fellow men
Like brutes within an iron den;
But what were these to us or him?
These wasted not his heart or limb;
My brother's soul was of that mold
Which in a palace had grown cold,
Had his free breathing been denied
The range of the steep mountain's side;
But why delay the truth?—he died.
I saw, and could not hold his head,
Nor reach his dying hand—nor dead,—
Though hard I strove, but strove in vain,
To rend and gnash my bonds in twain.
He died, and they unlocked his chain,
And scooped for him a shallow grave
Even from the cold earth of our cave.
I begged them as a boon to lay
His corse in dust whereon the day
Might shine—it was a foolish thought,

But then within my brain it wrought,
That even in death his freeborn breast
In such a dungeon could not rest.
I might have spared my idle prayer—
They coldly laughed, and laid him there:
The flat and turfless earth above
The being we so much did love;
His empty chain above it leant,
Such murder's fitting monument!

VIII

But he, the favorite and the flower,
Most cherished since his natal hour,
His mother's image in fair face,
The infant love of all his race,
His martyred father's dearest thought,
My latest care, for whom I sought
To hoard my life, that his might be
Less wretched now, and one day free;
He, too, who yet had held untired
A spirit natural or inspired—
He, too, was struck, and day by day
Was withered on the stalk away.
Oh, God! it is a fearful thing
To see the human soul take wing
In any shape, in any mood:
I've seen it rushing forth in blood,
I've seen it on the breaking ocean
Strive with a swoll'n convulsive motion,
I've seen the sick and ghastly bed
Of sin delirious with its dread;
But these were horrors—this was woe
Unmixed with such—but sure and slow:
He faded, and so calm and meek,
So softly worn, so sweetly weak,
So tearless, yet so tender, kind,
And grieved for those he left behind;
With all the while a cheek whose bloom

Was as a mockery of the tomb,
Whose tints as gently sunk away
As a departing rainbow's ray;
An eye of most transparent light,
That almost made the dungeon bright,
And not a word of murmur, not
A groan o'er his untimely lot,—
A little talk of better days,
A little hope my own to raise,
For I was sunk in silence—lost
In this last loss, of all the most;
And then the sighs he would suppress
Of fainting nature's feebleness,
More slowly drawn, grew less and less:
I listened, but I could not hear;
I called, for I was wild with fear;
I knew 'twas hopeless, but my dread
Would not be thus admonished;
I called, and thought I heard a sound—
I burst my chain with one strong bound,
And rushed to him:—I found him not,
I only stirred in this black spot,
I only lived, *I* only drew
The accursed breath of dungeon-dew;
The last, the sole, the dearest link
Between me and the eternal brink,
Which bound me to my failing race,
Was broken in this fatal place.
One on the earth, and one beneath—
My brothers—both had ceased to breathe:
I took that hand which lay so still,
Alas! my own was full as chill;
I had not strength to stir, or strive,
But felt that I was still alive—
A frantic feeling, when we know
That what we love shall ne'er be so.
I know not why
I could not die,

I had no earthly hope but faith,
And that forbade a selfish death.

IX

What next befell me then and there
    I know not well—I never knew—
First came the loss of light, and air,
    And then of darkness too:
I had no thought, no feeling—none—
Among the stones I stood a stone,
And was, scarce conscious what I wist,
As shrubless crags within the mist;
For all was blank, and bleak, and gray;
It was not night, it was not day;
It was not even the dungeon-light
So hateful to my heavy sight,
But vacancy absorbing space,
And fixedness without a place;
There were no stars, no earth, no time,
No check, no change, no good, no crime,
But silence, and a stirless breath
Which neither was of life nor death;
A sea of stagnant idleness,
Blind, boundless, mute, and motionless!

X

A light broke in upon my brain,—
    It was the carol of a bird;
It ceased, and then it came again,
    The sweetest song ear ever heard,
And mine was thankful till my eyes
Ran over with the glad surprise,
And they that moment could not see
I was the mate of misery;
But then by dull degrees came back
My senses to their wonted track;
I saw the dungeon walls and floor
Close slowly round me as before,

I saw the glimmer of the sun
Creeping as it before had done,
But through the crevice where it came
That bird was perched, as fond and tame,
    And tamer than upon the tree;
A lovely bird, with azure wings,
And song that said a thousand things,
    And seemed to say them all for me!
I never saw its like before,
I ne'er shall see its likeness more:
It seemed like me to want a mate,
But was not half so desolate,
And it was come to love me when
None lived to love me so again,
And cheering from my dungeon's brink,
Had brought me back to feel and think.
I know not if it late were free,
    Or broke its cage to perch on mine,
But knowing well captivity,
    Sweet bird! I could not wish for thine!
Or if it were, in winged guise,
A visitant from Paradise;
For–Heaven forgive that thought! the while
Which made me both to weep and smile–
I sometimes deemed that it might be
My brother's soul come down to me;
But then at last away it flew,
And then 'twas mortal well I knew,
For he would never thus have flown,
And left me twice so doubly lone,
Lone as the corse within its shroud,
Lone as a solitary cloud,–
    A single cloud on a sunny day,
While all the rest of heaven is clear,
A frown upon the atmosphere,
That hath no business to appear
    When skies are blue, and earth is gay.

XI

A kind of change came in my fate,
My keepers grew compassionate;
I know not what had made them so,
They were inured to sights of woe,
But so it was:—my broken chain
With links unfastened did remain,
And it was liberty to stride
Along my cell from side to side,
And up and down, and then athwart,
And tread it over every part;
And round the pillars one by one,
Returning where my walk begun,
Avoiding only, as I trod,
My brothers' graves without a sod;
For if I thought with heedless tread
My step profaned their lowly bed,
My breath came gaspingly and thick,
And my crushed heart felt blind and sick.

XII

I made a footing in the wall,
It was not therefrom to escape,
For I had buried one and all
Who loved me in a human shape;
And the whole earth would henceforth be
A wider prison unto me:
No child, no sire, no kin had I,
No partner in my misery;
I thought of this, and I was glad,
For thought of them had made me mad;
But I was curious to ascend
To my barred windows, and to bend

Once more, upon the mountains high,
The quiet of a loving eye.

XIII

I saw them, and they were the same,
They were not changed like me in frame;
I saw their thousand years of snow
On high—their wide long lake below,
And the blue Rhone in fullest flow;
I heard the torrents leap and gush
O'er channeled rock and broken bush;
I saw the white-walled distant town,
And whiter sails go skimming down;
And then there was a little isle,
Which in my very face did smile,
The only one in view;
A small green isle, it seemed no more,
Scarce broader than my dungeon floor,
But in it there were three tall trees,
And o'er it blew the mountain breeze,
And by it there were waters flowing,
And on it there were young flowers growing,
Of gentle breath and hue.
The fish swam by the castle wall,
And they seemed joyous each and all:
The eagle rode the rising blast,
Methought he never flew so fast
As then to me he seemed to fly;
And then new tears came in my eye,
And I felt troubled—and would fain
I had not left my recent chain;
And when I did descend again,
The darkness of my dim abode
Fell on me as a heavy load;
It was as is a new-dug grave,
Closing o'er one we sought to save,—
And yet my glance, too much oppressed,
Had almost need of such a rest.

XIV

It might be months, or years, or days,
  I kept no count, I took no note,
I had no hope my eyes to raise,
  And clear them of their dreary mote;
At last men came to set me free;
  I asked not why, and recked not where;
It was at length the same to me,
Fettered or fetterless to be,
  I learned to love despair.
And thus when they appeared at last,
And all my bonds aside were cast
These heavy walls to me had grown
A hermitage—and all my own!
And half I felt as they were come
To tear me from a second home:
With spiders I had friendship made,
And watched them in their sullen trade,
Had seen the mice by moonlight play,
And why should I feel less than they?
We were all inmates of one place,
And I, the monarch of each race,
Had power to kill—yet, strange to tell!
In quiet we had learned to dwell;
My very chains and I grew friends,
So much a long communion tends
To make us what we are:—even I
Regained my freedom with a sigh.

Percy Bysshe Shelley

ARETHUSA

Arethusa arose
From her couch of snows
In the Acroceraunian mountains,
From cloud and from crag,
With many a jag,
Shepherding her bright fountains.
She leapt down the rocks,
With her rainbow locks
Streaming among the streams;
Her steps paved with green
The downward ravine
Which slopes to the western gleams;
And gliding and springing
She went, ever singing,
In murmurs as soft as sleep;
The Earth seemed to love her,
And Heaven smiled above her,
As she lingered towards the deep.

Then Alpheus bold,
On his glacier cold,
With his trident the mountains strook;

And opened a chasm
In the rocks—with the spasm
All Erymanthus shook.
And the black south wind
It unsealed behind
The urns of the silent snow,
And earthquake and thunder
Did rend in sunder
The bars of the springs below.
And the beard and the hair
Of the River-god were
Seen through the torrent's sweep,
As he followed the light
Of the fleet nymph's flight
To the brink of the Dorian deep.

"Oh, save me! Oh, guide me!
And bid the deep hide me,
For he grasps me now by the hair!"
The loud Ocean heard,
To its blue depth stirred,
And divided at her prayer;
And under the water
The Earth's white daughter
Fled like a sunny beam;
Behind her descended
Her billows, unblended
With the brackish Dorian stream:
Like a gloomy stain
On the emerald main
Alpheus rushed behind,
As an eagle pursuing
A dove to its ruin
Down the streams of the cloudy wind.

Under the bowers
Where the Ocean powers
Sit on their pearled thrones;

Arethusa

Through the coral woods
Of the weltering floods,
Over heaps of unvalued stones;
Through the dim beams
Which amid the streams
Weave a network of colored light;
And under the caves,
Where the shadowy waves
Are as green as the forest's night:
Outspeeding the shark
And the sword-fish dark,
Under the Ocean's foam,
And up through the rifts
Of the mountain clifts
They passed to their Dorian home.

And now from their fountains
In Enna's mountains,
Down one vale where the morning basks,
Like friends once parted
Grown single-hearted,
They ply their watery tasks.
At sunrise they leap
From their cradles steep
In the cave of the shelving hill;
At noontide they flow
Through the woods below
And the meadows of asphodel;
And at night they sleep
In the rocking deep
Beneath the Ortygian shore;
Like spirits that lie
In the azure sky
When they love but live no more.

John Keats

THE EVE OF ST. AGNES

St. Agnes' Eve—Ah, bitter chill it was!
The owl, for all his feathers, was a-cold;
The hare limped trembling through the frozen grass,
And silent was the flock in woolly fold:
Numb were the Beadsman's fingers, while he told
His rosary, and while his frosted breath,
Like pious incense from a censer old,
Seemed taking flight for Heaven, without a death,
Past the sweet Virgin's picture, while his prayer he saith.

His prayer he saith, this patient, holy man;
Then takes his lamp, and riseth from his knees,
And back returneth, meager, barefoot, wan,
Along the chapel aisle by slow degrees:
The sculptured dead, on each side, seem to freeze,
Imprisoned in black, purgatorial rails:
Knights, ladies, praying in dumb orat'ries,
He passeth by; and his weak spirit fails
To think how they may ache in icy hoods and mails.

Northward he turneth through a little door,
And scarce three steps, ere music's golden tongue
Flattered to tears this aged man and poor;
But no—already had his deathbell rung:
The joys of all his life were said and sung:
His was harsh penance on St. Agnes' Eve:

Another way he went, and soon among
Rough ashes sat he for his soul's reprieve,
And all night kept awake, for sinners' sake to grieve.

That ancient Beadsman heard the prelude soft;
And so it chanced, for many a door was wide,
From hurry to and fro. Soon, up aloft,
The silver, snarling trumpets 'gan to chide:
The level chambers, ready with their pride,
Were glowing to receive a thousand guests:
The carved angels, ever eager-eyed,
Stared, where upon their heads the cornice rests,
With hair blown back and wings put cross-wise on their breasts.

At length burst in the argent revelry,
With plume, tiara, and all rich array,
Numerous as shadows haunting faerily
The brain, new stuffed, in youth, with triumphs gay
Of old romance. These let us wish away,
And turn, sole-thoughted, to one lady there,
Whose heart had brooded, all that wintry day,
On love, and winged St. Agnes' saintly care,
As she had heard old dames full many times declare.

They told her how, upon St. Agnes' Eve,
Young virgins might have visions of delight,
And soft adorings from their loves receive
Upon the honeyed middle of the night,
If ceremonies due they did aright;
As, supperless to bed they must retire,
And couch supine their beauties, lily white;
Nor look behind, nor sideways, but require
Of Heaven with upward eyes for all that they desire.

Full of this whim was thoughtful Madeline:
The music, yearning like a God in pain,
She scarcely heard: her maiden eyes divine,
Fixed on the floor, saw many a sweeping train

Pass by—she heeded not at all: in vain
Came many a tiptoe, amorous cavalier,
And back retired; not cooled by high disdain,
But she saw not: her heart was otherwhere:
She sighed for Agnes' dreams, the sweetest of the year.

She danced along with vague, regardless eyes,
Anxious her lips, her breathing quick and short:
The hallowed hour was near at hand: she sighs
Amid the timbrels, and the thronged resort
Of whisperers in anger, or in sport;
'Mid looks of love, defiance, hate, and scorn,
Hoodwinked with faery fancy; all amort,
Save to St. Agnes and her lambs unshorn,
And all the bliss to be before to-morrow morn.

So, purposing each moment to retire,
She lingered still. Meantime, across the moors,
Had come young Porphyro, with heart on fire
For Madeline. Beside the portal doors,
Buttressed from moonlight, stands he, and implores
All saints to give him sight of Madeline,
But for one moment in the tedious hours,
That he might gaze and worship all unseen;
Perchance speak, kneel, touch, kiss—in sooth such things have been.

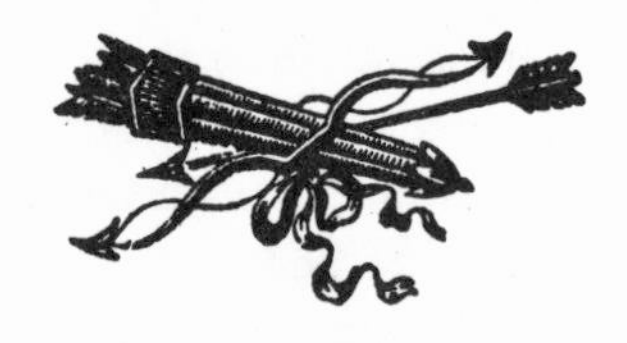

He ventures in: let no buzzed whisper tell:
All eyes be muffled, or a hundred swords
Will storm his heart, Love's fev'rous citadel:
For him, those chambers held barbarian hordes,
Hyena foemen, and hot-blooded lords,
Whose very dogs would execrations howl
Against his lineage: not one breast affords

Him any mercy, in that mansion foul,
Save one old beldame, weak in body and in soul.

Ah, happy chance! the aged creature came,
Shuffling along with ivory-headed wand,
To where he stood, hid from the torch's flame,
Behind a broad hall-pillar, far beyond
The sound of merriment and chorus bland:
He startled her; but soon she knew his face,
And grasped his fingers in her palsied hand,
Saying, "Mercy, Porphyro! hie thee from this place:
They are all here to-night, the whole blood-thirsty race!

"Get hence! get hence! there's dwarfish Hildebrand;
He had a fever late, and in the fit
He cursed thee and thine, both house and land:
Then there's that old Lord Maurice, not a whit
More tame for his gray hairs—Alas me! flit!
Flit like a ghost away."—"Ah, Gossip dear,
We're safe enough; here in this arm chair sit,
And tell me how"—"Good saints! not here, not here;
Follow me, child, or else these stones will be thy bier."

He followed through a lowly arched way,
Brushing the cobwebs with his lofty plume,
And as she muttered "Well-a—well-a-day!"
He found him in a little moonlight room,
Pale, latticed, chill, and silent as a tomb.
"Now tell me where is Madeline," said he,
"O tell me Angela, by the holy loom
Which none but secret sisterhood may see,
When they St. Agnes' wool are weaving piously."

"St. Agnes! Ah! it is St. Agnes' Eve—
Yet men will murder upon holy days:
Thou must hold water in a witch's sieve,
And be liege-lord of all the elves and fays,
To venture so: it fills me with amaze

To see thee, Porphyro!—St. Agnes' Eve!
God's help! my lady fair the conjuror plays
This very night: good angels her deceive!
But let me laugh awhile, I've mickle time to grieve."

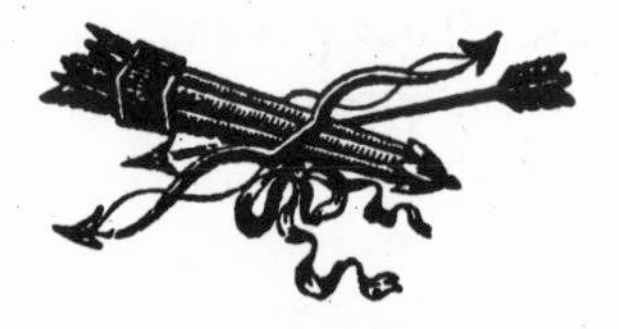

Feebly she laugheth in the languid moon,
While Porphyro upon her face doth look,
Like puzzled urchin on an aged crone
Who keepeth closed a wond'rous riddle-book,
As spectacled she sits in chimney nook.
But soon his eyes grew brilliant, when she told
His lady's purpose; and he scarce could brook
Tears, at the thought of those enchantments cold,
And Madeline asleep in lap of legends old.

Sudden a thought came like a full-blown rose,
Flushing his brow, and in his pained heart
Made purple riot: then doth he propose
A stratagem, that makes the beldame start:
"A cruel man and impious thou art:
Sweet lady, let her pray, and sleep, and dream
Alone with her good angels, far apart
From wicked men like thee. Go, go! I deem
Thou canst not surely be the same that thou didst seem."

"I will not harm her, by all saints I swear,"
Quoth Porphyro: "O may I ne'er find grace
When my weak voice shall whisper its last prayer,
If one of her soft ringlets I displace,
Or look with ruffian passion in her face:
Good Angela, believe me by these tears;
Or I will, even in a moment's space,
Awake, with horrid shout, my foemen's ears,
And beard them, though they be more fanged than wolves and bears."

"Ah! why wilt thou affright a feeble soul?
A poor, weak, palsy-stricken, churchyard thing,
Whose passing-bell may ere the midnight toll;
Whose prayers for thee, each morn and evening,
Were never missed." Thus plaining, doth she bring
A gentler speech from burning Porphyro;
So woeful, and of such deep sorrowing,
That Angela gives promise she will do
Whatever he shall wish, betide her weal or woe.

Which was, to lead him, in close secrecy,
Even to Madeline's chamber, and there hide
Him in a closet, of such privacy
That he might see her beauty unespied,
And win perhaps that night a peerless bride,
While legioned faeries paced the coverlet,
And pale enchantment held her sleepy-eyed.
Never on such a night have lovers met,
Since Merlin paid his Demon all the monstrous debt.

"It shall be as thou wishest," said the Dame:
"All cates and dainties shall be stored there
Quickly on this feast-night: by the tambour frame
Her own lute thou wilt see: no time to spare,
For I am slow and feeble, and scarce dare
On such a catering trust my dizzy head.
Wait here, my child, with patience; kneel in prayer
The while: Ah! thou must needs the lady wed,
Or may I never leave my grave among the dead."

So saying she hobbled off with busy fear.
The lover's endless minutes slowly passed;
The dame returned, and whispered in his ear
To follow her; with aged eyes aghast
From fright of dim espial. Safe at last,
Through many a dusky gallery, they gain
The maiden's chamber, silken, hushed, and chaste;

Where Porphyro took covert, pleased amain.
His poor guide hurried back with agues in her brain.

Her faltering hand upon the balustrade,
Old Angela was feeling for the stair,
When Madeline, St. Agnes' charmed maid,
Rose, like a missioned spirit, unaware:
With silver taper's light, and pious care,
She turned, and down the aged gossip led
To a safe level matting. Now prepare,
Young Porphyro, for gazing on that bed;
She comes, she comes again, like ring-dove frayed and fled.

Out went the taper as she hurried in;
Its little smoke, in pallid moonshine, died:
She closed the door, she panted, all akin
To spirits of the air, and visions wide:
No uttered syllable, or, woe betide!
But to her heart, her heart was voluble,
Paining with eloquence her balmy side;
As though a tongueless nightingale should swell
Her throat in vain, and die, heart-stifled, in her dell.

A casement high and triple-arched there was,
All garlanded with carven imag'ries
Of fruits, and flowers, and bunches of knot-grass,
And diamonded with panes of quaint device,
Innumerable of stains and splendid dyes,
As are the tiger-moth's deep-damasked wings;
And in the midst, 'mong thousand heraldries,
And twilight saints, and dim emblazonings,
A shielded scutcheon blushed with blood of queens and kings.

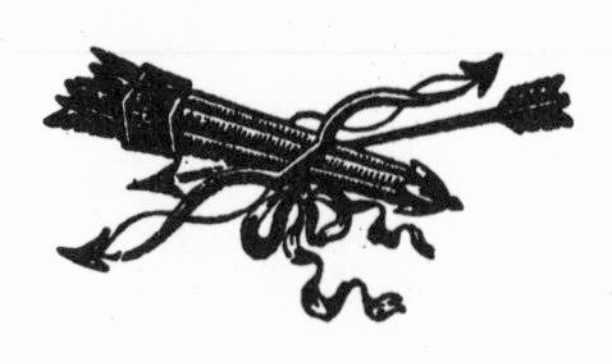

Full on this casement shone the wintry moon,
And threw warm gules on Madeline's fair breast,
As down she knelt for heaven's grace and boon;
Rose-bloom fell on her hands, together prest,
And on her silver cross soft amethyst,
And on her hair a glory, like a saint:
She seemed a splendid angel, newly drest,
Save wings, for heaven:—Porphyro grew faint:
She knelt, so pure a thing, so free from mortal taint.

Anon his heart revives: her vespers done,
Of all its wreathed pearls her hair she frees;
Unclasps her warmed jewels one by one;
Loosens her fragrant bodice; by degrees
Her rich attire creeps rustling to her knees:
Half-hidden like a mermaid in sea-weed,
Pensive awhile she dreams awake, and sees,
In fancy, fair St. Agnes in her bed,
But dares not look behind, or all the charm is fled.

Soon, trembling in her soft and chilly nest,
In sort of wakeful swoon, perplexed she lay,
Until the poppied warmth of sleep oppressed
Her soothed limbs, and soul fatigued away;
Flown, like a thought, until the morrow-day;
Blissfully havened both from joy and pain;
Clasped like a missal where swart Paynims pray;
Blinded alike from sunshine and from rain,
As though a rose should shut, and be a bud again.

Stol'n to this paradise, and so entranced,
Porphyro gazed upon her empty dress,
And listened to her breathing, if it chanced
To wake into a slumberous tenderness;
Which when he heard, that minute did he bless,
And breathed himself: then from the closet crept,
Noiseless as fear in a wide wilderness,

And over the hushed carpet, silent stepped,
And 'tween the curtains peeped, where, lo! how fast she slept.

Then by the bed-side where the faded moon,
Made a dim, silver twilight, soft he set
A table, and, half anguished, threw thereon
A cloth of woven crimson, gold, and jet:—
O for some drowsy Morphean amulet!
The boisterous, midnight, festive clarion,
The kettle-drum, and far-heard clarinet,
Affray his ears, though but in dying tone:—
The hall door shuts again, and all the noise is gone.

And still she slept an azure-lidded sleep,
In blanched linen, smooth, and lavendered,
While he from forth the closet brought a heap
Of candied apple, quince, and plum, and gourd;
With jellies soother than the creamy curd,
And lucent syrups, tinct with cinnamon;
Manna and dates, in argosy transferred
From Fez; and spiced dainties, every one,
From silken Samarcand to cedared Lebanon.

These delicates he heaped with glowing hand
On golden dishes and in baskets bright
Of wreathed silver: sumptuous they stand
In the retired quiet of the night,
Filling the chilly room with perfume light.—
"And now, my love, my seraph fair, awake!
Thou art my heaven, and I thine eremite:
Open thine eyes for meek St. Agnes' sake,
Or I shall drowse beside thee, so my soul doth ache."

Thus whispering, his warm, unnerved arm
Sank in her pillow. Shaded was her dream
By the dusk curtains: 'twas a midnight charm
Impossible to melt as iced stream:
The lustrous salvers in the moonlight gleam:

Broad golden fringe upon the carpet lies:
It seemed he never, never could redeem
From such a stedfast spell his lady's eyes;
So mused awhile, entoiled in woofed phantasies.

Awakening up, he took her hollow lute,—
Tumultuous,—and, in chords that tenderest be,
He played an ancient ditty, long since mute,
In Provence called, "La belle dame sans mercy":
Close to her ear touching the melody;
Wherewith disturbed, she uttered a soft moan:
He ceased—she panted quick—and suddenly
Her blue affrayed eyes wide open shone:
Upon his knees he sank, pale as smooth-sculptured stone.

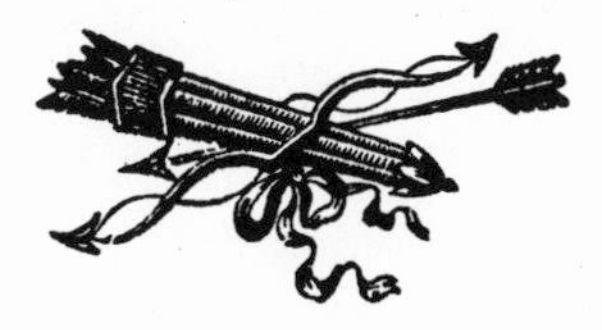

Her eyes were open, but she still beheld,
Now wide awake, the vision of her sleep.
There was a painful change, that nigh expelled
The blisses of her dream so pure and deep
At which fair Madeline began to weep,
And moan forth witless words with many a sigh;
While still her gaze on Porphyro would keep;
Who knelt, with joined hand, and piteous eye,
Fearing to move or speak, she looked so dreamingly.

"Ah, Porphyro!" said she, "but even now
Thy voice was at sweet tremble in mine ear,
Made tuneable with every sweetest vow;
And those sad eyes were spiritual and clear:
How changed thou art! how pallid, chill, and drear!
Give me that voice again, my Porphyro,
Those looks immortal, those complainings dear!
Oh leave me not in this eternal woe,
For if thou diest, my Love, I know not where to go."

Beyond a mortal man impassioned far
At these voluptuous accents, he arose,
Ethereal, flushed, and like a throbbing star
Seen mid the sapphire heaven's deep repose;
Into her dream he melted, as the rose
Blendeth its odor with the violet,—
Solution sweet: meantime the frost-wind blows
Like Love's alarum pattering the sharp sleet
Against the window-panes: St. Agnes' moon hath set.

'Tis dark: quick pattereth the flaw-blown sleet:
"This is no dream, my bride, my Madeline!"
'Tis dark: the iced gusts still rave and beat:
"No dream, alas! alas! and woe is mine!
Porphyro will leave me here to fade and pine.
Cruel! what traitor could thee hither bring?
I curse not, for my heart is lost in thine,
Though thou forsakest a deceived thing;
A dove forlorn and lost with sick unpruned wing."

"My Madeline! sweet dreamer! lovely bride!
Say, may I be for aye thy vassal blest?
Thy beauty's shield, heart-shaped and vermeil dyed?
Ah, silver shrine, here will I take my rest
After so many hours of toil and quest,
A famished pilgrim,—saved by miracle.
Though I have found, I will not rob thy nest
Saving of thy sweet self; if thou think'st well
To trust, fair Madeline, to no rude infidel.

"Hark! 'tis an elfin-storm from faery land,
Of haggard seeming, but a boon indeed:
Arise! arise! the morning is at hand;
The bloated wassaillers will never heed:
Let us away, my love, with happy speed;
There are no ears to hear, or eyes to see,—
Drowned all in Rhenish and the sleepy mead:
Awake! arise! my love, and fearless be,
For o'er the southern moors I have a home for thee."

She hurried at his words, beset with fears,
For there were sleeping dragons all around,
At glaring watch, perhaps, with ready spears—
Down the wide stairs a darkling way they found.
In all the house was heard no human sound.
A chain-drooped lamp was flickering by each door;
The arras, rich with horseman, hawk, and hound,
Fluttered in the besieging wind's uproar;
And the long carpets rose along the gusty floor.

They glide, like phantoms, into the wide hall;
Like phantoms, to the iron porch they glide;
Where lay the Porter, in uneasy sprawl,
With a huge empty flagon by his side:
The wakeful bloodhound rose, and shook his hide,
But his sagacious eye an inmate owns:
By one, and one, the bolts full easy slide:
The chains lie silent on the footworn stones;
The key turns, and the door upon its hinges groans.

And they are gone: ay, ages long ago
These lovers fled away into the storm.
That night the Baron dreamt of many a woe,
And all his warrior-guests, with shade and form
Of witch, and demon, and large coffin-worm,
Were long be-nightmared. Angela the old
Died palsy-twitched, with meager face deform;
The Beadsman, after thousand aves told,
For aye unsought for slept among his ashes cold.

John Keats

LA BELLE DAME SANS MERCI

"O what can ail thee, knight-at-arms,
Alone and palely loitering?
The sedge is withered from the lake,
And no birds sing.

"O what can ail thee, knight-at-arms,
So haggard and so woe-begone?
The squirrel's granary is full,
And the harvest's done.

"I see a lily on thy brow
With anguish moist and fever dew;
And on thy cheek a fading rose
Fast withereth too."

"I met a lady in the meads,
Full beautiful—a faery's child,
Her hair was long, her foot was light,
And her eyes were wild.

"I made a garland for her head,
And bracelets too, and fragrant zone;

She looked at me as she did love,
And made sweet moan.

"I set her on my pacing steed
And nothing else saw all day long,
For sideways would she lean, and sing
A faery's song.

"She found me roots of relish sweet,
And honey wild and manna dew,
And sure in language strange she said,
'I love thee true!'

"She took me to her elfin grot,
And there she wept and sighed full sore,
And there I shut her wild, wild eyes
With kisses four.

"And there she lulled me asleep,
And there I dreamed—Ah! woe betide!
The latest dream I ever dreamed
On the cold hill's side.

"I saw pale kings and princes too,
Pale warriors, death-pale were they all;
Who cried—'La belle Dame sans Merci
Hath thee in thrall!'

"I saw their starved lips in the gloam
With horrid warning gaped wide,
And I awoke and found me here
On the cold hill's side.

"And this is why I sojourn here
Alone and palely loitering,
Though the sedge is withered from the lake,
And no birds sing."

LADY GERALDINE'S COURTSHIP

A Romance of the Age

A Poet writes to his Friend. PLACE–A Room in Wycombe Hall.
TIME–Late in the evening.

I

Dear my friend and fellow-student, I would lean my spirit o'er you!
Down the purple of this chamber tears should scarcely run at will.
I am humbled who was humble. Friend, I bow my head before you:
You should lead me to my peasants, but their faces are too still.

II

There's a lady, an earl's daughter,–she is proud and she is noble,
And she treads the crimson carpet and she breathes the perfumed air,
And a kingly blood sends glances up, her princely eye to trouble,
And the shadow of a monarch's crown is softened in her hair.

III

She has halls among the woodlands, she has castles by the breakers,
She has farms and she has manors, she can threaten and command:

And the palpitating engines snort in steam across her acres,
As they mark upon the blasted heaven the measure of the land.

IV

There are none of England's daughters who can show a prouder presence;
Upon princely suitors' praying she has looked in her disdain.
She was sprung of English nobles, I was born of English peasants;
What was *I* that I should love her, save for competence to pain?

V

I was only a poor poet, made for singing at her casement,
As the finches or the thrushes, while she thought of other things.
Oh, she walked so high above me, she appeared to my abasement,
In her lovely silken murmur, like an angel clad in wings!

VI

Many vassals bow before her as her carriage sweeps their doorways;
She has blessed their little children, as a priest or queen were she:
Far too tender, or too cruel far, her smile upon the poor was,
For I thought it was the same smile which she used to smile on *me*.

VII

She has voters in the Commons, she has lovers in the palace,
And, of all the fair court-ladies, few have jewels half as fine;
Oft the Prince has named her beauty 'twixt the red wine and the chalice:
Oh, and what was *I* to love her? my beloved, my Geraldine!

VIII

Yet I could not choose but love her: I was born to poet-uses,
To love all things set above me, all of good and all of fair.
Nymphs of mountain, not of valley, we are wont to call the Muses;
And in nympholeptic climbing, poets pass from mount to star.

IX

And because I was a poet, and because the public praised me,
With a critical deduction for the modern writer's fault,
I could sit at rich men's tables,—though the courtesies that raised me,
Still suggested clear between us the pale spectrum of the salt.

X

And they praised me in her presence—"Will your book appear this summer?"
Then returning to each other—"Yes, our plans are for the moors."
Then with whisper dropped behind me—"There he is! the latest comer.
Oh, she only likes his verses! what is over, she endures.

XI

"Quite low-born, self-educated! somewhat gifted though by nature,
And we make a point of asking him,—of being very kind.
You may speak, he does not hear you! and, besides, he writes no satire,—
All these serpents kept by charmers leave the natural sting behind."

XII

I grew scornfuller, grew colder, as I stood up there among them,
Till as frost intense will burn you, the cold scorning scorched my brow;
When a sudden silver speaking, gravely cadenced, over-rung them,
And a sudden silken stirring touched my inner nature through.

XIII

I looked upward and beheld her: with a calm and regnant spirit,
Slowly round she swept her eyelids, and said clear before them all—
"Have you such superfluous honor, sir, that able to confer it
You will come down, Mister Bertram, as my guest to Wycombe Hall?"

XIV

Here she paused; she had been paler at the first word of her speaking,
But, because a silence followed it, blushed somewhat, as for shame:
Then, as scorning her own feeling, resumed calmly—"I am seeking
More distinction than these gentlemen think worthy of my claim.

XV

"Ne'ertheless, you see, I seek it—not because I am a woman,"
(Here her smile sprang like a fountain and, so, overflowed her mouth)
"But because my woods in Sussex have some purple shades at gloaming
Which are worthy of a king in state, or poet in his youth.

XVI

'I invite you, Mister Bertram, to no scene for worldly speeches—
Sir, I scarce should dare—but only where God asked the thrushes first:
And if *you* will sing beside them, in the covert of my beeches,
I will thank you for the woodlands,—for the human world, at worst."

XVII

Then she smiled around right childly, then she gazed around right queenly,
And I bowed—I could not answer; alternated light and gloom—
While as one who quells the lions, with a steady eye serenely,
She, with level fronting eyelids, passed out stately from the room.

XVIII

Oh, the blessed woods of Sussex, I can hear them still around me,
With their leafy tide of greenery still rippling up the wind!
Oh, the cursed woods of Sussex! where the hunter's arrow found me,
When a fair face and a tender voice had made me mad and blind!

XIX

In that ancient hall of Wycombe thronged the numerous guests invited,
And the lovely London ladies trod the floors with gliding feet;
And their voices low with fashion, not with feeling, softly freighted
All the air about the windows with elastic laughters sweet.

XX

For at eve the open windows flung their light out on the terrace
Which the floating orbs of curtains did with gradual shadow sweep,
While the swans upon the river, fed at morning by the heiress,
Trembled downward through their snowy wings at music in their sleep.

XXI

And there evermore was music, both of instrument and singing,
Till the finches of the shrubberies grew restless in the dark;
But the cedars stood up motionless, each in a moonlight's ringing,
And the deer, half in the glimmer, strewed the hollows of the park.

XXII

And though sometimes she would bind me with her silver-corded speeches
To commix my words and laughter with the converse and the jest,
Oft I sat apart and, gazing on the river through the beeches,
Heard, as pure the swans swam down it, her pure voice o'erfloat the rest.

XXIII

In the morning, horn of huntsman, hoof of steed and laugh of rider,
Spread out cheery from the courtyard till we lost them in the hills,
While herself and other ladies, and her suitors left beside her,
Went a-wandering up the gardens through the laurels and abeles.

XXIV

Thus, her foot upon the new-mown grass, bareheaded, with the flowing
Of the virginal white vesture gathered closely to her throat,
And the golden ringlets in her neck just quickened by her going,
And appearing to breathe sun for air, and doubting if to float,–

XXV

With a bunch of dewy maple, which her right hand held above her,
And which trembled a green shadow in betwixt her and the skies,
As she turned her face in going, thus, she drew me on to love her,
And to worship the divineness of the smile hid in her eyes.

XXVI

For her eyes alone smile constantly; her lips have serious sweetness,
And her front is calm, the dimple rarely ripples on the cheek;
But her deep blue eyes smile constantly, as if they in discreetness
Kept the secret of a happy dream she did not care to speak.

XXVII

Thus she drew me the first morning, out across into the garden,
And I walked among her noble friends and could not keep behind.
Spake she unto all and unto me–"Behold, I am the warden
Of the song-birds in these lindens, which are cages to their mind.

XXVIII

"But within this swarded circle into which the lime-walk brings us,
Whence the beeches, rounded greenly, stand away in reverent fear,

I will let no music enter, saving what the fountain sings us
Which the lilies round the basin may seem pure enough to hear.

XXIX

"The live air that waves the lilies waves the slender jet of water
Like a holy thought sent feebly up from soul of fasting saint:
Whereby lies a marble Silence, sleeping (Lough the sculptor wrought her),
So asleep she is forgetting to say Hush!—a fancy quaint.

XXX

"Mark how heavy white her eyelids! not a dream between them lingers;
And the left hand's index droppeth from the lips upon the cheek:
While the right hand,—with the symbol-rose held slack within the fingers,—
Has fallen backward in the basin—yet this Silence will not speak!

XXXI

"That the essential meaning growing may exceed the special symbol,
Is the thought as I conceive it: it applies more high and low.
Our true noblemen will often through right nobleness grow humble,
And assert an inward honor by denying outward show."

XXXII

"Nay, your Silence," said I, "truly, holds her symbol-rose but slackly,
Yet *she holds it*, or would scarcely be a Silence to our ken:
And your nobles wear their ermine on the outside, or walk blackly
In the presence of the social law as mere ignoble men.

XXXIII

"Let the poets dream such dreaming! madam, in these British islands
'Tis the substance that wanes ever, 'tis the symbol that exceeds.
Soon we shall have nought but symbol: and, for statues like this Silence,
Shall accept the rose's image—in another case, the weed's."

XXXIV

"Not so quickly," she retorted,—"I confess, where'er you go, you
Find for things, names—shows for actions, and pure gold for honor clear:

But when all is run to symbol in the Social, I will throw you
The world's book which now reads dryly, and sit down with Silence here."

XXXV

Half in playfulness she spoke, I thought, and half in indignation;
Friends, who listened, laughed her words off, while her lovers deemed her fair:
A fair woman, flushed with feeling, in her noble-lighted station
Near the statue's white reposing—and both bathed in sunny air!

XXXVI

With the trees round, not so distant but you heard their vernal murmur,
And beheld in light and shadow the leaves in and outward move,
And the little fountain leaping toward the sun-heart to be warmer,
Then recoiling in a tremble from the too much light above.

XXXVII

'Tis a picture for remembrance. And thus, morning after morning,
Did I follow as she drew me by the spirit to her feet.
Why, her greyhound followed also! dogs—we both were dogs for scorning—
To be sent back when she pleased it and her path lay through the wheat.

XXXVIII

And thus, morning after morning, spite of vows and spite of sorrow,
Did I follow at her drawing, while the week-days passed along,—
Just to feed the swans this noontide, or to see the fawns to-morrow,
Or to teach the hill-side echo some sweet Tuscan in a song.

XXXIX

Ay, for sometimes on the hill-side, while we sate down in the gowans,
With the forest green behind us and its shadow cast before,
And the river running under, and across it from the rowans
A brown partridge whirring near us till we felt the air it bore,—

XL

There, obedient to her praying, did I read aloud the poems
Made to Tuscan flutes, or instruments more various of our own;
Read the pastoral parts of Spenser, or the subtle interflowings
Found in Petrarch's sonnets—here's the book, the leaf is folded down!

XLI

Or at times a modern volume, Wordsworth's solemn-thoughted idyl,
Howitt's ballad-verse, or Tennyson's enchanted reverie,—
Or from Browning's some 'Pomegranate,' which, if cut deep down the middle,
Shows a heart within blood-tinctured, of a veined humanity.

XLII

Or at times I read there, hoarsely, some new poem of my making:
Poets ever fail in reading their own verses to their worth,
For the echo in you breaks upon the words which you are speaking,
And the chariot wheels jar in the gate through which you drive them forth.

XLIII

After, when we were grown tired of books, the silence round us flinging
A slow arm of sweet compression, felt with beatings at the breast,
She would break out on a sudden in a gush of woodland singing,
Like a child's emotion in a god—a naiad tired of rest.

XLIV

Oh, to see or hear her singing! scarce I know which is divinest,
For her looks sing too—she modulates her gestures on the tune,
And her mouth stirs with the song, like song; and when the notes are finest,
'Tis the eyes that shoot out vocal light and seem to swell them on.

XLV

Then we talked—oh, how we talked! her voice, so cadenced in the talking,
Made another singing—of the soul! a music without bars:
While the leafy sounds of woodlands, humming round where we were walking,
Brought interposition worthy-sweet,—as skies about the stars.

XLVI

And she spake such good thoughts natural, as if she always thought them;
She had sympathies so rapid, open, free as bird on branch,
Just as ready to fly east as west, whichever way besought them,
In the birchen-wood a chirrup, or a cock-crow in the grange.

XLVII

In her utmost lightness there is truth—and often she speaks lightly,
Has a grace in being gay which even mournful souls approve,
For the root of some grave earnest thought is understruck so rightly
As to justify the foliage and the waving flowers above.

XLVIII

And she talked on—*we* talked, rather! upon all things, substance, shadow,
Of the sheep that browsed the grasses, of the reapers in the corn,
Of the little children from the schools, seen winding through the meadow,
Of the poor rich world beyond them, still kept poorer by its scorn.

XLIX

So, of men, and so, of letters—books are men of higher stature,
And the only men that speak aloud for future times to hear;
So, of mankind in the abstract, which grows slowly into nature,
Yet will lift the cry of "progress," as it trod from sphere to sphere.

L

And her custom was to praise me when I said,—"The Age culls simples,
With a broad clown's back turned broadly to the glory of the stars.
We are gods by our own reck'ning, and may well shut up the temples,
And wield on, amid the incense-steam, the thunder of our cars.

LI

"For we throw out acclamations of self-thanking, self-admiring,
With, at every mile run faster,—'O the wondrous wondrous age!'
Little thinking if we work our souls as nobly as our iron,
Or if angels will command us at the goal of pilgrimage.

LII

"Why, what *is* this patient entrance into nature's deep resources
But the child's most gradual learning to walk upright without bane!
When we drive out, from the cloud of steam, majestical white horses,
Are we greater than the first men who led black ones by the mane?

LIII

"If we trod the deeps of ocean, if we struck the stars in rising,
If we wrapped the globe intensely with one hot electric breath,
'T were but power within our tether, no new spirit-power comprising,
And in life we were not greater men, nor bolder men in death."

LIV

She was patient with my talking; and I loved her, loved her certes
As I loved all heavenly objects, with uplifted eyes and hands;
As I loved pure inspirations, loved the graces, loved the virtues,
In a Love content with writing his own name on desert sands.

LV

Or at least I thought so, purely; thought no idiot Hope was raising
Any crown to crown Love's silence, silent Love that sate alone:
Out, alas! the stag is like me, he that tries to go on grazing
With the great deep gun-wound in his neck, then reels with sudden moan.

LVI

It was thus I reeled. I told you that her hand had many suitors;
But she smiles them down imperially as Venus did the waves,
And with such a gracious coldness that they cannot press their futures
On the present of her courtesy, which yieldingly enslaves.

LVII

And this morning as I sat alone within the inner chamber
With the great saloon beyond it, lost in pleasant thought serene,
For I had been reading Camoëns, that poem you remember,
Which his lady's eyes are praised in as the sweetest ever seen.

LVIII

And the book lay open, and my thought flew from it, taking from it
A vibration and impulsion to an end beyond its own,

As the branch of a green osier, when a child would overcome it,
Springs up freely from his claspings and goes swinging in the sun.

LIX

As I mused I heard a murmur; it grew deep as it grew longer,
Speakers using earnest language—"Lady Geraldine, you *would!*"
And I heard a voice that pleaded, ever on in accents stronger,
As a sense of reason gave it power to make its rhetoric good.

LX

Well I knew that voice, it was an earl's, of soul that matched his station,
Soul completed into lordship, might and right read on his brow;
Very finely courteous; far too proud to doubt his domination
Of the common people, he atones for grandeur by a bow.

LXI

High straight forehead, nose of eagle, cold blue eyes of less expression
Than resistance, coldly casting off the looks of other men,
As steel, arrows; unelastic lips which seem to taste possession
And be cautious lest the common air should injure or distrain.

LXII

For the rest, accomplished, upright,—ay, and standing by his order
With a bearing not ungraceful; fond of art and letters too;
Just a good man made a proud man,—as the sandy rocks that border
A wild coast, by circumstances, in a regnant ebb and flow.

LXIII

Thus, I knew that voice, I heard it, and I could not help the hearkening:
In the room I stood up blindly, and my burning heart within
Seemed to seethe and fuse my senses till they ran on all sides darkening,
And scorched, weighed like melted metal round my feet that stood therein.

LXIV

And that voice, I heard it pleading, for love's sake, for wealth, position,
For the sake of liberal uses and great actions to be done:

And she interrupted gently, "Nay, my lord, the old tradition
Of your Normans, by some worthier hand than mine is, should be won."

LXV

"Ah, that white hand!" he said quickly,–and in his he either drew it
Or attempted–for with gravity and instance she replied,
"Nay, indeed, my lord, this talk is vain, and we had best eschew it
And pass on, like friends, to other points less easy to decide."

LXVI

What he said again, I know not: it is likely that his trouble
Worked his pride up to the surface, for she answered in slow scorn,
"And your lordship judges rightly. Whom I marry shall be noble,
Ay, and wealthy. I shall never blush to think how he was born."

LXVII

There, I maddened! her words stung me. Life swept through me into fever,
And my soul sprang up astonished, sprang full-statured in an hour.
Know you what it is when anguish, with apocalyptic NEVER,
To a Pythian height dilates you, and despair sublimes to power?

LXVIII

From my brain the soul-wings budded, waved a flame about my body,
Whence conventions coiled to ashes. I felt self-drawn out, as man,
From amalgamate false natures, and I saw the skies grow ruddy
With the deepening feet of angels, and I knew what spirits can.

LXIX

I was mad, inspired–say either! (anguish worketh inspiration)
Was a man or beast–perhaps so, for the tiger roars when speared;
And I walked on, step by step along the level of my passion–
Oh my soul! and passed the doorway to her face, and never feared.

LXX

He had left her, peradventure, when my footstep proved my coming,
But for *her*–she half arose, then sate, grew scarlet and grew pale.
Oh, she trembled! 't is so always with a worldly man or woman
In the presence of true spirits; what else *can* they do but quail?

LXXI

Oh, she fluttered like a tame bird, in among its forest brothers
Far too strong for it; then drooping, bowed her face upon her hands;
And I spake out wildly, fiercely, brutal truths of her and others:
I, she planted in the desert, swathed her, windlike, with my sands.

LXXII

I plucked up her social fictions, bloody-rooted though leaf-verdant,
Trod them down with words of shaming,—all the purple and the gold,
All the "landed stakes" and lordships, all that spirits pure and ardent
Are cast out of love and honor because chancing not to hold.

LXXIII

"For myself I do not argue," said I, "though I love you, madam,
But for better souls that nearer to the height of yours have trod:
And this age shows, to my thinking, still more infidels to Adam
Than directly, by profession, simple infidels to God.

LXXIV

"Yet, O God," I said, "O grave," I said, "O mother's heart and bosom,
With whom first and last are equal, saint and corpse and little child!
We are fools to your deductions, in these figments of heart-closing;
We are traitors to your causes, in these sympathies defiled.

LXXV

"Learn more reverence, madam, not for rank or wealth—*that* needs no learning:
That comes quickly, quick as sin does, ay, and culminates to sin;
But for Adam's seed, MAN! Trust me, 't is a clay above your scorning,
With God's image stamped upon it, and God's kindling breath within.

LXXVI

"What right have you, madam, gazing your palace mirror daily,
Getting so by heart your beauty which all others must adore,
While you draw the golden ringlets down your fingers, to vow gaily
You will wed no man that's only good to God, and nothing more?

LXXVII

"Why what right have you, made fair by that same God, the sweetest woman
Of all women He has fashioned, with your lovely spirit-face
Which would seem too near to vanish if its smile were not so human,
And your voice of holy sweetness, turning common words to grace,—

LXXVIII

"What right *can* you have, God's other works to scorn, despise, revile them
In the gross, as mere men, broadly—not as *noble* men, forsooth,—
As mere Pariahs of the outer world, forbidden to assoil them
In the hope of living, dying, near that sweetness of your mouth?

LXXIX

"Have you any answer, madam? If my spirit were less earthly,
If its instrument were gifted with a better silver string,
I would kneel down where I stand, and say—Behold me! I am worthy
Of thy loving, for I love thee. I am worthy as a king.

LXXX

"As it is—your ermined pride, I swear, shall feel this stain upon her,
That *I*, poor, weak, tost with passion, scorned by me and you again,
Love you, madam, dare to love you, to my grief and your dishonor,
To my endless desolation, and your impotent disdain!"

LXXXI

More mad words like these—mere madness! friend, I need not write them fuller,
For I hear my hot soul dropping on the lines in showers of tears,
Oh, a woman! friend, a woman! why, a beast had scarce been duller
Than roar bestial loud complaints against the shining of the spheres.

LXXXII

But at last there came a pause. I stood all vibrating with thunder
Which my soul had used. The silence drew her face up like a call.
Could you guess what word she uttered? She looked up, as if in wonder,
With tears beaded on her lashes, and said—"Bertram!"—It was all.

LXXXIII

If she had cursed me, and she might have, or if even, with queenly bearing
Which at need is used by women, she had risen up and said,
"Sir, you are my guest, and therefore I have given you a full hearing:
Now, beseech you, choose a name exacting somewhat less, instead!"—

LXXXIV

I had borne it: but that "Bertram"—why, it lies there on the paper
A mere word, without her accent, and you cannot judge the weight
Of the calm which crushed my passion: I seemed drowning in a vapor;
And her gentleness destroyed me whom her scorn made desolate.

LXXXV

So, struck backward and exhausted by that inward flow of passion
Which had rushed on, sparing nothing, into forms of abstract truth,
By a logic agonizing through unseemly demonstration,
And by youth's own anguish turning grimly gray the hairs of youth,—

LXXXVI

By the sense accursed and instant, that if even I spake wisely
I spake basely—using truth, if what I spake indeed was true,
To avenge wrong on a woman—*her*, who sate there weighing nicely
A poor manhood's worth, found guilty of such deeds as I could do!—

LXXXVII

By such wrong and woe exhausted—what I suffered and occasioned,—
As a wild horse through a city runs with lightning in his eyes,
And then dashing at a church's cold and passive wall, impassioned,
Strikes the death into his burning brain, and blindly drops and dies—

LXXXVIII

So I fell, struck down before her—do you blame me, friend, for weakness?
'T was my strength of passion slew me!—fell before her like a stone;
Fast the dreadful world rolled from me on its roaring wheels of blackness:
When the light came I was lying in this chamber and alone.

LXXXIX

Oh, of course she charged her lacqueys to bear out the sickly burden,
And to cast it from her scornful sight, but not *beyond* the gate;

She is too kind to be cruel, and too haughty not to pardon
Such a man as I; 't were something to be level to her hate.

XC

But for me—you now are conscious why, my friend, I write this letter,
How my life is read all backward, and the charm of life undone.
I shall leave her house at dawn; I would to-night, if I were better—
And I charge my soul to hold my body strengthened for the sun.

XCI

When the sun has dyed the oriel, I depart, with no last gazes,
No weak moanings (one word only, left in writing for her hands),
Out of reach of all derision, and some unavailing praises,
To make front against this anguish in the far and foreign lands.

XCII

Blame me not. I would not squander life in grief—I am abstemious.
I but nurse my spirit's falcon that its wing may soar again.
There's no room for tears of weakness in the blind eyes of a Phemius:
Into work the poet kneads them, and he does not die *till then.*

Conclusion

I

Bertram finished the last pages, while along the silence ever
Still in hot and heavy splashes fell the tears on every leaf.
Having ended, he leans backward in his chair, with lips that quiver
From the deep unspoken, ay, and deep unwritten thoughts of grief.

II

Soh! how still the lady standeth! 'T is a dream—a dream of mercies!
'Twixt the purple lattice-curtains how she standeth still and pale!
'T is a vision, sure, of mercies, sent to soften his self-curses,
Sent to sweep a patient quiet o'er the tossing of his wail.

III

"Eyes," he said, "now throbbing through me! are ye eyes that did undo me?
Shining eyes, like antique jewels set in Parian statue-stone!
Underneath that calm white forehead are ye ever burning torrid
O'er the desolate sand-desert of my heart and life undone?"

IV

With a murmurous stir uncertain, in the air the purple curtain
Swelleth in and swelleth out around her motionless pale brows,
While the gliding of the river sends a rippling noise for ever
Through the open casement whitened by the moonlight's slant repose.

V

Said he—"Vision of a lady! stand there silent, stand there steady!
Now I see it plainly, plainly now I cannot hope or doubt—
There, the brows of mild repression—there, the lips of silent passion,
Curved like an archer's bow to send the bitter arrows out."

VI

Ever, evermore the while in a slow silence she kept smiling,
And approached him slowly, slowly, in a gliding measured pace;
With her two white hands extended as if praying one offended,
And a look of supplication gazing earnest in his face.

VII

Said he—"Wake me by no gesture,—sound of breath, or stir of vesture!
Let the blessed apparition melt not yet to its divine!
No approaching—hush, no breathing! or my heart must swoon to death in
The too utter life thou bringest, O thou dream of Geraldine!"

VIII

Ever, evermore the while in a slow silence she kept smiling,
But the tears ran over lightly from her eyes and tenderly:—
"Dost thou, Bertram, truly love me? Is no woman far above me
Found more worthy of thy poet-heart than such a one as *I*?"

IX

Said he—"I would dream so ever, like the flowing of that river,
Flowing ever in a shadow greenly onward to the sea!

So, thou vision of all sweetness, princely to a full completeness
Would my heart and life flow onward, deathward, through this dream of
THEE!"

X

Ever, evermore the while in a slow silence she kept smiling,
While the silver tears ran faster down the blushing of her cheeks;
Then with both her hands enfolding both of his, she softly told him,
"Bertram, if I say I love thee, . . . 't is the vision only speaks."

XI

Softened, quickened to adore her, on his knee he fell before her,
And she whispered low in triumph, "It shall be as I have sworn.
Very rich he is in virtues, very noble–noble, certes;
And I shall not blush in knowing that men call him lowly born."

Lord Tennyson

MORTE D'ARTHUR

So all day long the noise of battle rolled
Among the mountains by the winter sea;
Until King Arthur's table, man by man,
Had fall'n in Lyonnesse about their Lord,
King Arthur: then, because his wound was deep,
The bold Sir Bedivere uplifted him,
Sir Bedivere, the last of all his knights,
And bore him to a chapel nigh the field,
A broken chancel with a broken cross,
That stood on a dark strait of barren land.
On one side lay the Ocean, and on one
Lay a great water, and the moon was full.
    Then spake King Arthur to Sir Bedivere:
"The sequel of to-day unsolders all
The goodliest fellowship of famous knights
Whereof this world holds record. Such a sleep
They sleep—the men I loved. I think that we
Shall never more, at any future time,
Delight our souls with talk of knightly deeds,
Walking about the gardens and the halls
Of Camelot, as in the days that were.

I perish by this people which I made,—
Tho' Merlin sware that I should come again
To rule once more—but let what will be, be.
I am so deeply smitten thro' the helm
That without help I cannot last till morn.
Thou therefore take my brand Excalibur,
Which was my pride: for thou rememberest how
In those old days, one summer noon, an arm
Rose up from out the bosom of the lake,
Clothed in white samite, mystic, wonderful,
Holding the sword—and how I rowed across
And took it, and have worn it, like a king:
And, wheresoever I am sung or told
In aftertime, this also shall be known:
But now delay not: take Excalibur,
And fling him far into the middle mere:
Watch what thou seest, and lightly bring me word."
To him replied the bold Sir Bedivere:
"It is not meet, Sir King, to leave thee thus,
Aidless, alone, and smitten thro' the helm.
A little thing may harm a wounded man.
Yet I thy hest will all perform at full,
Watch what I see, and lightly bring thee word."
So saying, from the ruined shrine he stepped
And in the moon athwart the place of tombs,
Where lay the mighty bones of ancient men,
Old knights, and over them the sea-wind sang
Shrill, chill, with flakes of foam. He, stepping down
By zig-zag paths, and juts of pointed rock,
Came on the shining levels of the lake.
There drew he forth the brand Excalibur,
And o'er him, drawing it, the winter moon,
Brightening the skirts of a long cloud, ran forth
And sparkled keen with frost against the hilt:
For all the haft twinkled with diamond sparks,
Myriads of topaz-lights, and jacinth-work
Of subtlest jewelery. He gazed so long
That both his eyes were dazzled, as he stood,

This way and that dividing the swift mind,
In act to throw: but at the last it seemed
Better to leave Excalibur concealed
There in the many-knotted waterflags,
That whistled stiff and dry about the marge.
So strode he back slow to the wounded King.
Then spake King Arthur to Sir Bedivere:
"Hast thou performed my mission which I gave?
What is it thou has seen? or what hast heard?"
And answer made the bold Sir Bedivere:
"I heard the ripple washing in the reeds,
And the wild water lapping on the crag."
To whom replied King Arthur, faint and pale:
"Thou hast betrayed thy nature and thy name,
Not rendering true answer, as beseemed
Thy fealty, nor like a noble knight:
For surer sign had followed, either hand,
Or voice, or else a motion of the mere.
This is a shameful thing for men to lie.
Yet now, I charge thee, quickly go again
As thou art lief and dear, and do the thing
I bade thee, watch, and lightly bring me word."
Then went Sir Bedivere the second time
Across the ridge, and paced beside the mere,
Counting the dewy pebbles, fixed in thought;
But when he saw the wonder of the hilt,
How curiously and strangely chased, he smote
His palms together, and he cried aloud,
"And if indeed I cast the brand away,
Surely a precious thing, one worthy note,
Should thus be lost for ever from the earth,
Which might have pleased the eyes of many men.
What good should follow this, if this were done?
What harm, undone? deep harm to disobey,
Seeing obedience is the bond of rule.
Were it well to obey then, if a king demand
An act unprofitable, against himself?
The King is sick, and knows not what he does.

What record, or what relic of my lord
Should be to aftertime, but empty breath
And rumors of a doubt? But were this kept,
Stored in some treasure-house of mighty kings,
Some one might show it at a joust of arms,
Saying, 'King Arthur's sword, Excalibur,
Wrought by the lonely maiden of the Lake,
Nine years she wrought it, sitting in the deeps
Upon the hidden bases of the hills.'
So might some old man speak in the aftertime
To all the people, winning reverence.
But now much honor and much fame were lost."
    So spake he, clouded with his own conceit,
And hid Excalibur the second time,
And so strode back slow to the wounded King.

    Then spoke King Arthur, breathing heavily:
"What is it thou hast seen? or what hast heard?"
    And answer made the bold Sir Bedivere:
"I heard the water lapping on the crag,
And the long ripple washing in the reeds."
    To whom replied King Arthur, much in wrath:
"Ah, miserable and unkind, untrue,
Unknightly, traitor-hearted! Woe is me!
Authority forgets a dying king,
Laid widowed of the power in his eye
That bowed the will. I see thee what thou art,
For thou, the latest-left of all my knights,
In whom should meet the offices of all,
Thou wouldst betray me for the precious hilt;
Either from lust of gold, or like a girl
Valuing the giddy pleasure of the eyes.
Yet, for a man may fail in duty twice,

And the third time may prosper, get thee hence:
But, if thou spare to fling Excalibur,
I will arise and slay thee with my hands."
  Then quickly rose Sir Bedivere, and ran,
And, leaping down the ridges lightly, plunged
Among the bulrush-beds, and clutched the sword,
And strongly wheeled and threw it. The great brand
Made lightnings in the splendor of the moon,
And flashing round and round, and whirled in an arch,
Shot like a streamer of the northern morn,
See where the moving isles of winter shock
By night, with noises of the northern sea.
So flashed and fell the brand Excalibur:
But ere he dipped the surface, rose an arm
Clothed in white samite, mystic, wonderful,
And caught him by the hilt, and brandished him
Three times, and drew him under in the mere.
And lightly went the other to the King.
    Then spoke King Arthur, drawing thicker breath:
"Now see I by thine eyes that this is done.
Speak out: what is it thou hast heard, or seen?"
    And answer made the bold Sir Bedivere:
"Sir King, I closed mine eyelids, lest the gems
Should blind my purpose, for I never saw,
Nor shall see, here or elsewhere, till I die,
Not tho' I live three lives of mortal men,
So great a miracle as yonder hilt.
Then with both hands I flung him, wheeling him:
But when I looked again, behold an arm,
Clothed in white samite, mystic, wonderful,
That caught him by the hilt, and brandished him
Three times, and drew him under in the mere."
    And answer made King Arthur, breathing hard:
"My end draws nigh: 'tis time that I were gone.
Make broad thy shoulders to receive my weight,
And bear me to the margin; yet I fear
My wound hath taken cold, and I shall die."
    So saying, from the pavement he half rose,

Slowly, with pain, reclining on his arm,
And looking wistfully with wide blue eyes
As in a picture. Him Sir Bedivere
Remorsefully regarded thro' his tears,
And would have spoken, but he found not words,
Then took with care, and kneeling on one knee,
O'er both his shoulders drew the languid hands,
And rising bore him thro' the place of tombs.

But, as he walked, King Arthur panted hard,
Like one that feels a nightmare on his bed
When all the house is mute. So sighed the King,
Muttering and murmuring at his ear, "Quick, quick!
I fear it is too late, and I shall die."
But the other swiftly strode from ridge to ridge,
Clothed with his breath, and looking, as he walked,
Larger than human on the frozen hills.
He heard the deep behind him, and a cry
Before. His own thought drove him like a goad.
Dry clashed his harness in the icy caves
And barren chasms, and all to left and right
The bare black cliff clanged round him, as he based
His feet on juts of slippery crag that rang
Sharp-smitten with the dint of armed heels–
And on a sudden, lo! the level lake,
And the long glories of the winter moon.

Then saw they how there hove a dusky barge,
Dark as a funeral scarf from stem to stern,
Beneath them; and descending they were ware
That all the decks were dense with stately forms
Black-stoled, black-hooded, like a dream–by these
Three Queens with crowns of gold–and from them rose
A cry that shivered to the tingling stars,
And, as it were one voice, an agony
Of lamentation, like a wind, that shrills
All night in a waste land, where no one comes,
Or hath come, since the making of the world.

Then murmured Arthur, "Place me in the barge,"
And to the barge they came. There those three Queens

Put forth their hands, and took the King, and wept.
But she, that rose the tallest of them all
And fairest, laid his head upon her lap,
And loosed the shattered casque, and chafed his hands,
And called him by his name, complaining loud,
And dropping bitter tears against his brow
Striped with dark blood: for all his face was white
And colorless, and like the withered moon
Smote by the fresh beam of the springing east;
And all his greaves and cuisses dashed with drops
Of onset; and the light and lustrous curls—
That made his forehead like a rising sun
High from the dais-throne—were parched with dust;
Or, clotted into points and hanging loose,
Mixed with the knightly growth that fringed his lips.
So like a shattered column lay the King;
Not like that Arthur who, with lance in rest,
From spur to plume a star of tournament,
Shot through the lists at Camelot, and charged
Before the eyes of ladies and of kings.

Then loudly cried the bold Sir Bedivere,
"Ah! my Lord Arthur, whither shall I go?
Where shall I hide my forehead and my eyes?
For now I see the true old times are dead,
When every morning brought a noble chance,
And every chance brought out a noble knight.
Such times have been not since the light that led
The holy Elders with the gift of myrrh.
But now the whole Round Table is dissolved
Which was an image of the mighty world;
And I, the last, go forth companionless,
And the days darken round me, and the years,
Among new men, strange faces, other minds."

And slowly answered Arthur from the barge:
"The old order changeth, yielding place to new,
And God fulfils Himself in many ways,
Lest one good custom should corrupt the world.
Comfort thyself: what comfort is in me?
I have lived my life, and that which I have done
May He within Himself make pure! but thou,
If thou shouldst never see my face again,
Pray for my soul. More things are wrought by prayer
Than this world dreams of. Wherefore, let thy voice
Rise like a fountain for me night and day.
For what are men better than sheep or goats
That nourish a blind life within the brain,
If, knowing God, they lift not hands of prayer
Both for themselves and those who call them friend?
For so the whole round earth is every way
Bound by gold chains about the feet of God.
But now farewell. I am going a long way
With these thou seest—if indeed I go—
(For all my mind is clouded with a doubt)
To the island-valley of Avilion;
Where falls not hail, or rain, or any snow,
Nor ever wind blows loudly; but it lies
Deep-meadowed, happy, fair with orchard-lawns
And bowery hollows crowned with summer sea,
Where I will heal me of my grievous wound."
So said he, and the barge with oar and sail
Moved from the brink, like some full-breasted swan
That, fluting a wild carol ere her death,
Ruffles her pure cold plume, and takes the flood
With swarthy webs. Long stood Sir Bedivere
Revolving many memories, till the hull
Looked one black dot against the verge of dawn,
And on the mere the wailing died away.

THE REVENGE

A Ballad of the Fleet

I

At Flores in the Azores Sir Richard Grenville lay,
And a pinnace, like a fluttered bird, came flying from far away:
"Spanish ships of war at sea! we have sighted fifty-three!"
Then sware Lord Thomas Howard: " 'Fore God I am no coward;
But I cannot meet them here, for my ships are out of gear,
And the half my men are sick. I must fly, but follow quick.
We are six ships of the line; can we fight with fifty-three?"

II

Then spake Sir Richard Grenville: "I know you are no coward;
You fly them for a moment to fight with them again.
But I've ninety men and more that are lying sick ashore.
I should count myself the coward if I left them, my Lord Howard,
To these Inquisition dogs and the devildoms of Spain."

III

So Lord Howard passed away with five ships of war that day,
Till he melted like a cloud in the silent summer heaven;
But Sir Richard bore in hand all his sick men from the land
Very carefully and slow,
Men of Bideford in Devon,
And we laid them on the ballast down below;
For we brought them all aboard,
And they blessed him in their pain, that they were not left to Spain,
To the thumb-screw and the stake, for the glory of the Lord.

IV

He had only a hundred seamen to work the ship and to fight,
And he sailed away from Flores till the Spaniard came in sight,
With his huge sea-castles heaving upon the weather bow.
"Shall we fight or shall we fly?
Good Sir Richard, tell us now,
For to fight is but to die!
There'll be little of us left by the time this sun be set."
And Sir Richard said again: "We be all good English men.
Let us bang these dogs of Seville, the children of the devil,
For I never turned my back upon Don or devil yet."

V

Sir Richard spoke and he laughed, and we roared a hurrah, and so
The little *Revenge* ran on sheer into the heart of the foe,
With her hundred fighters on deck, and her ninety sick below;
For half of their fleet to the right and half to the left were seen,
And the little *Revenge* ran on through the long sea-lane between.

VI

Thousands of their soldiers looked down from their decks and laughed,
Thousands of their seamen made mock at the mad little craft
Running on and on, till delayed
By their mountain-like *San Philip* that, of fifteen hundred tons,
And up-shadowing high above us with her yawning tiers of guns,
Took the breath from our sails, and we stayed.

VII

And while now the great *San Philip* hung above us like a cloud
Whence the thunderbolt will fall
Long and loud,
Four galleons drew away
From the Spanish fleet that day,
And two upon the larboard and two upon the starboard lay,
And the battle-thunder broke from them all.

VIII

But anon the great *San Philip*, she bethought herself and went,
Having that within her womb that had left her ill content;
And the rest they came aboard us, and they fought us hand to hand,
For a dozen times they came with their pikes and musketeers,
And a dozen times we shook 'em off as a dog that shakes his ears
When he leaps from the water to the land.

IX

And the sun went down, and the stars came out far over the summer sea,
But never a moment ceased the fight of the one and the fifty-three.
Ship after ship, the whole night long, their high-built galleons came,
Ship after ship, the whole night long, with her battle-thunder and flame;
Ship after ship, the whole night long, drew back with her dead and her shame.
For some were sunk and many were shattered, and so could fight us no more–
God of battles, was ever a battle like this in the world before?

X

For he said, "Fight on! fight on!"
Though his vessel was all but a wreck;
And it chanced that, when half of the short summer night was gone,
With a grisly wound to be dressed he had left the deck,
But a bullet struck him that was dressing it suddenly dead,
And himself he was wounded again in the side and the head,
And he said, "Fight on! fight on!"

XI

And the night went down, and the sun smiled out far over the summer sea,
And the Spanish fleet with broken sides lay round us all in a ring;
But they dared not touch us again, for they feared that we still could sting,
So they watched what the end would be.
And we had not fought them in vain,
But in perilous plight were we,
Seeing forty of our poor hundred were slain,
And half of the rest of us maimed for life
In the crash of the cannonades and the desperate strife;
And the sick men down in the hold were most of them stark and cold,
And the pikes were all broken or bent, and the powder was all of it spent;
And the masts and the rigging were lying over the side;
But Sir Richard cried in his English pride:
"We have fought such a fight for a day and a night
As may never be fought again!
We have won great glory, my men!
And a day less or more
At sea or ashore,
We die—does it matter when?
Sink me the ship, Master Gunner—sink her, split her in twain!
Fall into the hands of God, not into the hands of Spain!"

XII

And the gunner said, "Ay, ay," but the seamen made reply:
"We have children, we have wives,
And the Lord hath spared our lives.
We will make the Spaniard promise, if we yield, to let us go;
We shall live to fight again and to strike another blow."
And the lion there lay dying, and they yielded to the foe.

XIII

And the stately Spanish men to their flagship bore him then,
Where they laid him by the mast, old Sir Richard caught at last,
And they praised him to his face with their courtly foreign grace;
But he rose upon their decks, and he cried:
"I have fought for Queen and Faith like a valiant man and true;
I have only done my duty as a man is bound to do.

With a joyful spirit I Sir Richard Grenville die!"
And he fell upon their decks, and he died.

XIV

And they stared at the dead that had been so valiant and true,
And had holden the power and glory of Spain so cheap
That he dared her with one little ship and his English few;
Was he devil or man? He was devil for aught they knew,
But they sank his body with honor down into the deep,
And they manned the *Revenge* with a swarthier alien crew,
And away she sailed with her loss and longed for her own;
When a wind from the lands they had ruined awoke from sleep,
And the water began to heave and the weather to moan,
And or ever that evening ended a great gale blew,
And a wave like the wave that is raised by an earthquake grew,
Till it smote on their hulls and their sails and their masts and their flags,
And the whole sea plunged and fell on the shot-shattered navy of Spain,
And the little *Revenge* herself went down by the island crags
To be lost evermore in the main.

Robert Browning

SOLILOQUY OF THE SPANISH CLOISTER

I

Gr-r-r—there go, my heart's abhorrence!
    Water your damned flower-pots, do!
If hate killed men, Brother Lawrence,
    God's blood, would not mine kill you!
What? your myrtle-bush wants trimming?
    Oh, that rose has prior claims—
Needs its leaden vase filled brimming?
    Hell dry you up with its flames!

II

At the meal we sit together:
    Salve tibi! I must hear
Wise talk of the kind of weather,
    Sort of season, time of year:
Not a plenteous cork-crop: scarcely
    Dare we hope oak-galls, I doubt:
What's the Latin name for 'parsley'?
    What's the Greek name for Swine's Snout?

III

Whew! We'll have our platter burnished,
Laid with care on our own shelf!
With a fire-new spoon we're furnished,
And a goblet for ourself,
Rinsed like something sacrificial
Ere 'tis fit to touch our chaps–
Marked with L. for our initial!
(He-he! There his lily snaps!)

IV

Saint, forsooth! While brown Dolores
Squats outside the Convent bank,
With Sanchicha, telling stories,
Steeping tresses in the tank,
Blue-black, lustrous, thick like horse-hairs,
–Can't I see his dead eye glow,
Bright as 'twere a Barbary corsair's?
(That is, if he'd let it show!)

V

When he finishes refection,
Knife and fork he never lays
Cross-wise, to my recollection,
As do I, in Jesu's praise.
I, the Trinity illustrate,
Drinking watered orange-pulp–
In three sips the Arian frustrate;
While he drains his at one gulp!

VI

Oh, those melons! If he's able
We're to have a feast; so nice!
One goes to the Abbot's table,
All of us get each a slice.
How go on your flowers? None double?
Not one fruit-sort can you spy?
Strange!–And I, too, at such trouble,
Keep them close-nipped on the sly!

VII

There's a great text in Galatians,
    Once you trip on it, entails
Twenty-nine distinct damnations,
    One sure, if another fails:
If I trip him just a-dying,
    Sure of Heaven as sure as can be,
Spin him round and send him flying
    Off to Hell, a Manichee?

VIII

Or, my scrofulous French novel
    On grey paper with blunt type!
Simply glance at it, you grovel
    Hand and foot in Belial's gripe:
If I double down its pages
    At the woeful sixteenth print,
When he gathers his greengages,
    Ope a sieve and slip it in't?

IX

Or, there's Satan!—one might venture
    Pledge one's soul to him, yet leave
Such a flaw in the indenture
    As he'd miss till, past retrieve,
Blasted lay that rose-acacia
    We're so proud of! *Hy, Zy, Hine* . . .
'St, there's Vespers! *Plena gratiâ*
    Ave, Virgo! Gr-r-r—you swine!

Robert Browning

"CHILDE ROLAND TO THE DARK TOWER CAME"

(See Edgar's song in "LEAR"*)*

My first thought was, he lied in every word,
    That hoary cripple, with malicious eye
    Askance to watch the working of his lie
On mine, and mouth scarce able to afford
Suppression of the glee that pursed and scored
    Its edge at one more victim gained thereby.

What else should he be set for, with his staff?
    What, save to waylay with his lies, ensnare
    All travelers that might find him posted there,
And ask the road? I guessed what skull-like laugh
Would break, what crutch 'gin write my epitaph
    For pastime in the dusty thoroughfare,

If at his counsel I should turn aside
    Into that ominous tract which, all agree,
    Hides the Dark Tower. Yet acquiescingly

I did turn as he pointed; neither pride
Nor hope rekindling at the end descried,
    So much as gladness that some end might be.

For, what with my whole world-wide wandering,
    What with my search drawn out thro' years, my hope
    Dwindled into a ghost not fit to cope
With that obstreperous joy success would bring,—
I hardly tried now to rebuke the spring
    My heart made, finding failure in its scope.

As when a sick man very near to death
    Seems dead indeed, and feels begin and end
    The tears and takes the farewell of each friend,
And hears one bid the other go, draw breath
Freelier outside, ("since all is o'er," he saith,
    "And the blow fallen no grieving can amend;")

While some discuss if near the other graves
    Be room enough for this, and when a day
    Suits best for carrying the corpse away,
With care about the banners, scarves and staves,—
And still the man hears all, and only craves
    He may not shame such tender love and stay.

Thus, I had so long suffered in this quest,
    Heard failure prophesied so oft, been writ
    So many times among "The Band"—to wit,
The knights who to the Dark Tower's search addressed
Their steps—that just to fail as they, seemed best,
    And all the doubt was now—should I be fit.

So, quiet as despair, I turned from him,
    That hateful cripple, out of his highway
    Into the path he pointed. All the day
Had been a dreary one at best, and dim
Was settling to its close, yet shot one grim
    Red leer to see the plain catch its estray.

For mark! no sooner was I fairly found
Pledged to the plain, after a pace or two,
Than, pausing to throw backward a last view
To the safe road, 'twas gone; gray plain all round:
Nothing but plain to the horizon's bound.
I might go on; nought else remained to do.

So, on I went. I think I never saw
Such starved ignoble nature; nothing throve:
For flowers—as well expect a cedar grove!
But cockle, spurge, according to their law
Might propagate their kind, with none to awe,
You'd think; a burr had been a treasure-trove.

No! penury, inertness and grimace,
In some strange sort, were the land's portion. "See
Or shut your eyes," said Nature peevishly,
"It nothing skills: I cannot help my case:
'Tis the Last Judgment's fire must cure this place,
Calcine its clods and set my prisoners free."

If there pushed any ragged thistle-stalk
Above its mates, the head was chopped—the bents
Were jealous else. What made those holes and rents
In the dock's harsh swarth leaves—bruised as to balk
All hope of greenness? 'tis a brute must walk
Pashing their life out, with a brute's intents.

As for the grass, it grew as scant as hair
In leprosy; thin dry blades pricked the mud
Which underneath looked kneaded up with blood.
One stiff blind horse, his every bone a-stare,
Stood stupefied, however he came there:
Thrust out past service from the devil's stud!

Alive? he might be dead for aught I know,
With that red, gaunt and colloped neck a-strain,
And shut eyes underneath the rusty mane;

Seldom went such grotesqueness with such woe;
I never saw a brute I hated so;
    He must be wicked to deserve such pain.

I shut my eyes and turned them on my heart.
    As a man calls for wine before he fights,
    I asked one draught of earlier, happier sights,
Ere fitly I could hope to play my part.
Think first, fight afterwards—the soldier's art:
    One taste of the old time sets all to rights!

Not it! I fancied Cuthbert's reddening face
    Beneath its garniture of curly gold,
    Dear fellow, till I almost felt him fold
An arm in mine to fix me to the place,
That way he used. Alas, one night's disgrace!
  Out went my heart's new fire and left it cold.

Giles, then, the soul of honor—there he stands
    Frank as ten years ago when knighted first.
    What honest men should dare (he said) he durst.
Good—but the scene shifts—faugh! what hangman's hands
Pin to his breast a parchment? his own bands
    Read it. Poor traitor, spit upon and curst!

Better this Present than a Past like that;
    Back therefore to my darkening path again.
    No sound, no sight as far as eye could strain.
Will the night send a howlet or a bat?
I asked: when something on the dismal flat
    Came to arrest my thoughts and change their train.

A sudden little river crossed my path
    As unexpected as a serpent comes.
    No sluggish tide congenial to the glooms—
This, as it frothed by, might have been a bath
For the fiend's glowing hoof—to see the wrath
    Of its black eddy bespate with flakes and spumes.

So petty yet so spiteful! all along,
    Low scrubby alders kneeled down over it;
    Drenched willows flung them headlong in a fit
Of mute despair, a suicidal throng:
The river which had done them all the wrong,
    Whate'er that was, rolled by, deterred no whit.

Which, while I forded,–good saints, how I feared
    To set my foot upon a dead man's cheek,
    Each step, or feel the spear I thrust to seek
For hollows, tangled in his hair or beard!
–It may have been a water-rat I speared,
    But, ugh! it sounded like a baby's shriek.

Glad was I when I reached the other bank.
    Now for a better country. Vain presage!
    Who were the strugglers, what war did they wage
Whose savage trample thus could pad the dank
Soil to a plash? toads in a poisoned tank,
    Or wild cats in a red-hot iron cage–

The fight must so have seemed in that fell cirque.
    What penned them there, with all the plain to choose?
    No foot-print leading to that horrid mews,
None out of it. Mad brewage set to work
Their brains, no doubt, like galley-slaves the Turk
    Pits for his pastime, Christians against Jews.

And more than that–a furlong on–why, there!
    What bad use was that engine for, that wheel,
    Or brake, not wheel–that harrow fit to reel
Men's bodies out like silk? with all the air
Of Tophet's tool, or earth left unaware,
    Or brought to sharpen its rusty teeth of steel.

Then came a bit of stubbed ground, once a wood,
    Next a marsh, it would seem, and now mere earth
    Desperate and done with; (so a fool finds mirth,

Makes a thing and then mars it, till his mood
Changes and off he goes!) within a rood—
Bog, clay and rubble, sand and stark black dearth.

Now blotches rankling, colored gay and grim,
Now patches where some leanness of the soil's
Broke into moss or substances like boils;
Then came some palsied oak, a cleft in him
Like a distorted mouth that splits its rim
Gaping at death, and dies while it recoils.

And just as far as ever from the end!
Nought in the distance but the evening, nought
To point my footstep further! At the thought,
A great black bird, Apollyon's bosom-friend,
Sailed past, nor beat his wide wing dragon-penned
That brushed my cap—perchance the guide I sought.

For, looking up, aware I somehow grew,
'Spite of the dusk, the plain had given place
All round to mountains—with such name to grace
Mere ugly heights and heaps now stolen in view.
How thus they had surprised me,—solve it, you!
How to get from them was no clearer case.

Yet half I seemed to recognize some trick
Of mischief happened to me, God knows when—
In a bad dream perhaps. Here ended, then,
Progress this way. When, in the very nick
Of giving up, one time more, came a click
As when a trap shuts—you're inside the den!

Burningly it came on me all at once,
This was the place! those two hills on the right,
Crouched like two bulls locked horn in horn in fight;
While to the left, a tall scalped mountain . . . Dunce,
Fool, to be dozing at the very nonce,
After a life spent training for the sight!

What in the midst lay but the Tower itself?
The round squat turret, blind as the fool's heart,
Built of brown stone, without a counterpart
In the whole world. The tempest's mocking elf
Points to the shipman thus the unseen shelf
He strikes on, only when the timbers start.

Not see? because of night perhaps?—Why, day
Came back again for that! before it left,
The dying sunset kindled through a cleft:
The hills, like giants at a hunting, lay,
Chin upon hand, to see the game at bay,—
"Now stab and end the creature—to the heft!"

Not hear? when noise was everywhere! it tolled
Increasing like a bell. Names in my ears,
Of all the lost adventurers my peers,—
How such a one was strong, and such was bold,
And such was fortunate, yet each of old
Lost, lost! one moment knelled the woe of years.

There they stood, ranged along the hillsides, met
To view the last of me, a living frame
For one more picture! in a sheet of flame
I saw them and I knew them all. And yet
Dauntless the slug-horn to my lips I set,
And blew. "*Childe Roland to the Dark Tower came.*"

Matthew Arnold

SOHRAB AND RUSTUM

An Episode

And the first gray of morning filled the east,
And the fog rose out of the Oxus stream.
But all the Tartar camp along the stream
Was hushed, and still the men were plunged in sleep;
Sohrab alone, he slept not; all night long
He had lain wakeful, tossing on his bed;
But when the gray dawn stole into his tent,
He rose, and clad himself, and girt his sword,
And took his horseman's cloak, and left his tent,
And went abroad into the cold wet fog,
Through the dim camp to Peran-Wisa's tent.

Through the black Tartar tents he passed, which stood
Clustering like bee-hives on the low flat strand
Of Oxus, where the summer floods o'erflow
When the sun melts the snows in high Pamere;
Through the black tents he passed, o'er that low strand,
And to a hillock came, a little back
From the stream's brink—the spot where first a boat,
Crossing the stream in summer, scrapes the land.

The men of former times had crowned the top
With a clay fort; but that was fall'n, and now
The Tartars built there Peran-Wisa's tent,
A dome of laths, and o'er it felts were spread.
And Sohrab came there, and went in, and stood
Upon the thick piled carpets in the tent,
And found the old man sleeping on his bed
Of rugs and felts, and near him lay his arms.
And Peran-Wisa heard him, though the step
Was dulled; for he slept light, an old man's sleep;
And he rose quickly on one arm, and said:
"Who art thou? for it is not yet clear dawn.
Speak! is there news, or any night alarm?"
But Sohrab came to the bedside, and said:
"Thou know'st me. Peran-Wisa! it is I.
The sun is not yet risen, and the foe
Sleep; but I sleep not; all night long I lie
Tossing and wakeful, and I come to thee.
For so did King Afrasiab bid me seek
Thy counsel, and to heed thee as thy son,
In Samarcand, before the army marched;
And I will tell thee what my heart desires.
Thou know'st if, since from Ader-baijan first
I came among the Tartars, and bore arms,
I have still served Afrasiab well, and shown,
At my boy's years, the courage of a man.
This too thou know'st, that, while I still bear on
The conquering Tartar ensigns through the world,
And beat the Persians back on every field,
I seek one man, one man, and one alone–
Rustum, my father; who, I hoped, should greet,
Should one day greet, upon some well-fought field
His not unworthy, not inglorious son.
So I long hoped, but him I never find.
Come then, hear now, and grant me what I ask.
Let the two armies rest to-day; but I
Will challenge forth the bravest Persian lords
To meet me, man to man: if I prevail,

Rustum will surely hear it; if I fall—
Old man, the dead need no one, claim no kin.
Dim is the rumor of a common fight,
Where host meets host, and many names are sunk;
But of a single combat fame speaks clear."
He spoke: and Peran-Wisa took the hand
Of the young man in his, and sighed, and said:
"O Sohrab, an unquiet heart is thine!
Canst thou not rest among the Tartar chiefs,
And share the battle's common chance with us
Who love thee, but must press for ever first,
In single fight incurring single risk,
To find a father thou hast never seen?
That were far best, my son, to stay with us
Unmurmuring; in our tents, while it is war,
And when 'tis truce, then in Afrasiab's towns.
But, if this one desire indeed rules all,
To seek out Rustum—seek him not through fight!
Seek him in peace, and carry to his arms,
O Sohrab, carry an unwounded son!
But far hence seek him, for he is not here.
For now it is not as when I was young,
When Rustum was in front of every fray;
But now he keeps apart, and sits at home,
In Seistan, with Zal, his father old.
Whether that his own mighty strength at last
Feels the abhorred approaches of old age;
Or in some quarrel with the Persian King.
There go!—Thou wilt not? Yet my heart forebodes
Danger or death awaits thee on this field.
Fain would I know thee safe and well, though lost
To us; fain therefore send thee hence, in peace
To seek thy father, not seek single fights
In vain;—but who can keep the lion's cub
From ravening? and who govern Rustum's son?
Go: I will grant thee what thy heart desires."
So said he, and dropped Sohrab's hand, and left
His bed, and the warm rugs whereon he lay,

And o'er his chilly limbs his woollen coat
He passed, and tied his sandals on his feet,
And threw a white cloak round him, and he took
In his right hand a ruler's staff, no sword;
And on his head he set his sheep-skin cap,
Black, glossy, curled, the fleece of Kara-Kul;
And raised the curtain of his tent, and called
His herald to his side, and went abroad.

The sun, by this, had risen, and cleared the fog
From the broad Oxus and the glittering sands.
And from their tents the Tartar horsemen filed
Into the open plain; so Haman bade—
Haman, who next to Peran-Wisa ruled
The host, and still was in his lusty prime.
From their black tents, long files of horse, they streamed:
As when, some gray November morn, the files,
In marching order spread, of long-necked cranes,
Stream over Casbin, and the southern slopes
Of Elburz, from the Aralian estuaries,
Or some frore Caspian reed-bed, southward bound
For the warm Persian sea-board—so they streamed.
The Tartars of the Oxus, the King's guard,
First with black sheep-skin caps and with long spears;
Large men, large steeds; who from Bokhara come
And Khiva, and ferment the milk of mares.
Next the more temperate Toorkmuns of the south,
The Tukas, and the lances of Salore,
And those from Attruck and the Caspian sands;
Light men, and on light steeds, who only drink
The acrid milk of camels, and their wells.
And then a swarm of wandering horse, who came
From far, and a more doubtful service owned;
The Tartars of Ferghana, from the banks
Of the Jaxartes, men with scanty beards
And close-set skull-caps; and those wilder hordes
Who roam o'er Kipchak and the northern waste,
Kalmuks and unkemped Kuzzaks, tribes who stray
Nearest the Pole, and wandering Kirghizzes,

Who come on shaggy ponies from Pamere;
These all filed out from camp into the plain.
And on the other side the Persians formed:
First a light cloud of horse, Tartars they seemed,
The Ilyats of Khorassan; and behind,
The royal troops of Persia, horse and foot,
Marshaled battalions bright in burnished steel.
But Peran-Wisa with his herald came
Threading the Tartar squadrons to the front,
And with his staff kept back the foremost ranks.
And when Ferood, who led the Persians, saw
That Peran-Wisa kept the Tartars back,
He took his spear, and to the front he came,
And checked his ranks, and fixed them where they stood.
And the old Tartar came upon the sand
Betwixt the silent hosts, and spake, and said:
"Ferood, and ye, Persians and Tartars, hear!
Let there be truce between the hosts to-day.
But choose a champion from the Persian lords
To fight our champion Sohrab, man to man."

As, in the country, on a morn in June,
When the dew glistens on the pearled ears,
A shiver runs through the deep corn for joy—
So, when they heard what Peran-Wisa said,
A thrill through all the Tartar squadrons ran
Of pride and hope for Sohrab, whom they loved.

But as a troop of pedlars, from Cabool,
Cross underneath the Indian Caucasus,
That vast sky-neighboring mountain of milk snow,
Winding so high, that, as they mount, they pass
Long flocks of traveling birds dead on the snow,
Choked by the air, and scarce can they themselves
Slake their parched throats with sugared mulberries—
In single file they move, and stop their breath,
For feat they should dislodge the o'erhanging snows—
So the pale Persians held their breath with fear.
And to Ferood his brother chiefs came up
To counsel: Gudurz and Zoarrah came,
And Feraburz, who ruled the Persian host
Second, and was the uncle of the King;
These came and counseled, and then Gudurz said:
"Ferood, shame bids us take their challenge up,
Yet champion have we none to match this youth.
He has the wild stag's foot, the lion's heart.
But Rustum came last night; aloof he sits
And sullen, and has pitched his tents apart:
Him will I seek, and carry to his ear
The Tartar challenge, and this young man's name.
Haply he will forget his wrath, and fight.
Stand forth the while, and take their challenge up."
So spake he; and Ferood stood forth and said:
"Old man, be it agreed as thou hast said.
Let Sohrab arm, and we will find a man."
He spake; and Peran-Wisa turned, and strode
Back through the opening squadrons to his tent.
But through the anxious Persians Gudurz ran,
And crossed the camp which lay behind, and reached,
Out on the sands beyond it, Rustum's tents.
Of scarlet cloth they were, and glittering gay,
Just pitched: the high pavilion in the midst
Was Rustum's, and his men lay camped around.
And Gudurz entered Rustum's tent, and found
Rustum; his morning meal was done, but still
The table stood before him, charged with food;

A side of roasted sheep, and cakes of bread,
And dark green melons; and there Rustum sate
Listless, and held a falcon on his wrist,
And played with it; but Gudurz came and stood
Before him; and he looked, and saw him stand,
And with a cry sprang up, and dropped the bird,
And greeted Gudurz with both hands, and said:

"Welcome! these eyes could see no better sight.
What news? but sit down first, and eat and drink."

But Gudurz stood in the tent-door, and said:
"Not now! a time will come to eat and drink,
But not to-day; to-day has other needs.
The armies are drawn out, and stand at gaze;
For from the Tartars is a challenge brought
To pick a champion from the Persian lords
To fight their champion—and thou know'st his name—
Sohrab men call him, but his birth is hid.
O Rustum, like thy might is this young man's!
He has the wild stag's foot, the lion's heart;
And he is young, and Iran's chiefs are old,
Or else too weak; and all eyes turn to thee.
Come down and help us, Rustum, or we lose!"

He spoke: but Rustum answered with a smile:
"Go to! if Iran's chiefs are old, then I
Am older: if the young are weak, the King
Errs strangely; for the King, for Kai Khosroo,
Himself is young, and honors younger men,
And lets the aged molder to their graves.
Rustum he loves no more, but loves the young—
The young may rise at Sohrab's vaunts, not I.
For what care I, though all speak Sohrab's fame?
For would that I myself had such a son,
And not that one slight helpless girl I have,
A son so famed, so brave, to send to war,
And I to tarry with the snow-haired Zal,
My father, whom the robber Afghans vex,
And clip his borders short, and drive his herds,
And he has none to guard his weak old age.

There would I go, and hang my armor up,
And with my great name fence that weak old man,
And spend the goodly treasures I have got,
And rest my age, and hear of Sohrab's fame,
And leave to death the hosts of thankless kings,
And with these slaughterous hands draw sword no more."
He spoke, and smiled; and Gudurz made reply:
"What then, O Rustum, will men say to this,
When Sohrab dares our bravest forth, and seeks
Thee most of all, and thou whom most he seeks,
Hidest thy face? Take heed, that men should say,
Like some old miser, Rustum hoards his fame,
And shuns to peril it with younger men."
And, greatly moved, then Rustum made reply:
"O Gudurz, wherefore dost thou say such words?
Thou knowest better words than this to say.
What is one more, one less, obscure or famed,
Valiant or craven, young or old, to me?
Are not they mortal, am not I myself?
But who for men of nought would do great deeds?
Come, thou shalt see how Rustum hoards his fame!
But I will fight unknown, and in plain arms;
Let not men say of Rustum, he was matched
In single fight with any mortal man."
He spoke, and frowned; and Gudurz turned and ran
Back quickly through the camp in fear and joy,
Fear at his wrath, but joy that Rustum came.
But Rustum strode to his tent door, and called
His followers in, and bade them bring his arms,
And clad himself in steel: the arms he chose
Were plain, and on his shield was no device,
Only his helm was rich, inlaid with gold,
And, from the fluted spine atop, a plume
Of horsehair waved, a scarlet horsehair plume.
So armed he isued forth; and Ruksh, his horse,
Followed him, like a faithful hound, at heel—
Ruksh, whose renown was noised through all the earth,
The horse, whom Rustum on a foray once

Did in Bokhara by the river find
A colt beneath its dam, and drove him home,
And reared him; a bright bay, with lofty crest;
Dight with a saddle-cloth of broidered green
Crusted with gold, and on the ground were worked
All beasts of chase, all beasts which hunters know.
So followed, Rustum left his tents, and crossed
The camp, and to the Persian host appeared.
And all the Persians knew him, and with shouts
Hailed; but the Tartars knew not who he was.
And dear as the wet diver to the eyes
Of his pale wife who waits and weeps on shore,
By sandy Bahrein, in the Persian Gulf,
Plunging all day in the blue waves, at night,
Having made up his tale of precious pearls,
Rejoins her in their hut upon the sands—
So dear to the pale Persians Rustum came.

And Rustum to the Persian front advanced,
And Sohrab armed in Haman's tent, and came.
And as afield the reapers cut a swath
Down through the middle of a rich man's corn,
And on each side are squares of standing corn,
And in the midst a stubble, short and bare—
So on each side were squares of men, with spears
Bristling, and in the midst, the open sand.
And Rustum came upon the sand, and cast
His eyes towards the Tartar tents, and saw
Sohrab come forth, and eyed him as he came.

As some rich woman, on a winter's morn,
Eyes through her silken curtains the poor drudge
Who with numb blackened fingers makes her fire—
At cock-crow, on a starlit winter's morn,
When the frost flowers the whitened window panes—
And wonders how she lives, and what the thoughts
Of that poor drudge may be; so Rustum eyed
The unknown adventurous youth, who from afar
Came seeking Rustum, and defying forth
All the most valiant chiefs: long he perused

His spirited air, and wondered who he was.
For very young he seemed, tenderly reared;
Like some young cypress, tall, and dark, and straight,
Which in a queen's secluded garden throws
Its slight dark shadow on the moonlit turf,
By midnight, to a bubbling fountain's sound—
So slender Sohrab seemed, so softly reared.
And a deep pity entered Rustum's soul
As he beheld him coming; and he stood,
And beckoned to him with his hand, and said:
"O thou young man, the air of Heaven is soft,
And warm, and pleasant; but the grave is cold!
Heaven's air is better than the cold dead grave.
Behold me! I am vast, and clad in iron,
And tried; and I have stood on many a field
Of blood, and I have fought with many a foe—
Never was that field lost, or that foe saved.
O Sohrab, wherefore wilt thou rush on death?
Be governed: quit the Tartar host, and come
To Iran, and be as my son to me,
And fight beneath my banner till I die!
There are no youths in Iran brave as thou."

So he spake, mildly: Sohrab heard his voice,
The mighty voice of Rustum, and he saw
His giant figure planted on the sand,
Sole, like some single tower, which a chief

Hath builded on the waste in former years
Against the robbers; and he saw that head,
Streaked with its first gray hairs–hope filled his soul,
And he ran forward and embraced his knees,
And clasped his hand within his own and said:
"Oh, by thy father's head! by thine own soul!
Art thou not Rustum? speak! art thou not he?"
But Rustum eyed askance the kneeling youth,
And turned away, and spake to his own soul:
"Ah me, I muse what this young fox may mean.
False, wily, boastful, are these Tartar boys.
For if I now confess this thing he asks,
And hide it not, but say: *Rustum is here!*
He will not yield indeed, nor quit our foes,
But he will find some pretext not to fight,
And praise my fame, and proffer courteous gifts,
A belt or sword perhaps, and go his way.
And on a feast-tide, in Afrasiab's hall,
In Samarcand, he will arise and cry:
'I challenged once, when the two armies camped
Beside the Oxus, all the Persian lords
To cope with me in single fight; but they
Shrank, only Rustum dared; then he and I
Changed gifts, and went on equal terms away.'
So will he speak, perhaps, while men applaud.
Then were the chiefs of Iran shamed through me."
And then he turned, and sternly spake aloud:
"Rise! wherefore dost thou vainly question thus
Of Rustum? I am here, whom thou hast called
By challenge forth; make good thy vaunt, or yield!
Is it with Rustum only thou wouldst fight?
Rash boy, men look on Rustum's face and flee.
For well I know, that did great Rustum stand
Before thy face this day, and were revealed
There would be then no talk of fighting more.
But being what I am, I tell thee this–
Do thou record it in thine inmost soul:
Either thou shalt renounce thy vaunt, and yield;

Or else thy bones shall strew this sand, till winds
Bleach them, or Oxus with his summer floods,
Oxus in summer wash them all away."

He spoke, and Sohrab answered, on his feet:
"Art thou so fierce? Thou wilt not fright me so!
I am no girl, to be made pale by words.
Yet this thou hast said well, did Rustum stand
Here on this field, there were no fighting then.
But Rustum is far hence, and we stand here.
Begin! thou art more vast, more dread than I,
And thou art proved, I know, and I am young—
But yet success sways with the breath of Heaven.
And though thou thinkest that thou knowest sure
Thy victory, yet thou canst not surely know.
For we are all, like swimmers in the sea,
Poised on the top of a huge wave of fate,
Which hangs uncertain to which side to fall.
And whether it will heave us up to land,
Or whether it will roll us out to sea,
Back out to sea, to the deep waves of death,
We know not, and no search will make us know;
Only the event will teach us in its hour."

He spoke; and Rustum answered not, but hurled
His spear; down from the shoulder, down it came,
As on some partridge in the corn a hawk
That long has towered in the airy clouds
Drops like a plummet; Sohrab saw it come,
And sprang aside, quick as a flash; the spear
Hissed, and went quivering down into the sand,
Which it sent flying wide;—then Sohrab threw
In turn, and full struck Rustum's shield; sharp rang,
The iron plates rang sharp, but turned the spear.
And Rustum seized his club, which none but he
Could wield; an unlopped trunk it was, and huge,
Still rough—like those which men in treeless plains
To build them boats fish from the flooded rivers,
Hyphasis or Hydaspes, when, high up
By their dark springs, the wind in winter-time

Has made in Himalayan forests wrack,
And strewn the channels with torn boughs—so huge
The club which Rustum lifted now, and struck
One stroke; but again Sohrab sprang aside
Lithe as the glancing snake, and the club came
Thundering to earth, and leapt from Rustum's hand.
And Rustum followed his own blow, and fell
To his knees, and with his fingers clutched the sand;
And now might Sohrab have unsheathed his sword,
And pierced the mighty Rustum while he lay
Dizzy, and on his knees, and choked with sand;
But he looked on, and smiled, nor bared his sword,
But courteously drew back, and spoke, and said:

"Thou strik'st too hard: that club of thine will float
Upon the summer floods, and not my bones.
But rise, and be not wroth! not wroth am I;
No, when I see thee, wrath forsakes my soul.
Thou say'st, thou are not Rustum; be it so!
Who art thou then, that canst so touch my soul?
Boy as I am, I have seen battles too—
Have waded foremost in their bloody waves,
And heard their hollow roar of dying men;
But never was my heart thus touched before.
Are they from Heaven, these softenings of the heart?
O thou old warrior, let us yield to Heaven!
Come, plant we here in earth our angry spears,
And make a truce, and sit upon this sand,
And pledge each other in red wine, like friends,
And thou shalt talk to me of Rustum's deeds.
There are enough foes in the Persian host
Whom I may meet, and strike, and feel no pang;
Champions enough Afrasiab has, whom thou
Mayst fight; fight *them*, when they confront thy spear!
But oh, let there be peace 'twixt thee and me!"

He ceased: but while he spake, Rustum had risen,
And stood erect, trembling with rage; his club
He left to lie, but had regained his spear,
Whose fiery point now in his mailed right-hand

Blazed bright and baleful, like that autumn-star,
The baleful sign of fevers; dust had soiled
His stately crest, and dimmed his glittering arms.
His breast heaved; his lips foamed; and twice his voice
Was choked with rage: at last these words broke way:
  "Girl! nimble with thy feet, not with thy hands!
Curled minion, dancer, coiner of sweet words!
Fight, let me hear thy hateful voice no more!
Thou art not in Afrasiab's gardens now
With Tartar girls, with whom thou art wont to dance;
But on the Oxus-sands, and in the dance
Of battle, and with me, who make no play
Of war; I fight it out, and hand to hand.
Speak not to me of truce, and pledge, and wine!
Remember all thy valor; try thy feints
And cunning! all the pity I had is gone;
Because thou hast shamed me before both the hosts
With thy light skipping tricks, and thy girl's wiles."
  He spoke; and Sohrab kindled at his taunts,
And he too drew his sword: at once they rushed
Together, as two eagles on one prey
Come rushing down together from the clouds,
One from the east, one from the west, their shields
Dashed with a clang together, and a din
Rose, such as that the sinewy woodcutters
Make often in the forest's heart at morn
Of hewing axes, crashing trees—such blows
Rustum and Sohrab on each other hailed.
And you would say that sun and stars took part
In that unnatural conflict; for a cloud
Grew suddenly in Heaven, and darked the sun
Over the fighters' heads; and a wind rose
Under their feet, and moaning swept the plain,
And in a sandy whirlwind wrapped the pair.
In gloom they twain were wrapped, and they alone;
For both the on-looking hosts on either hand
Stood in broad daylight, and the sky was pure,
And the sun sparkled on the Oxus stream.

But in the gloom they fought, with bloodshot eyes
And laboring breath; first Rustum struck the shield
Which Sohrab held stiff out; the steel-spiked spear
Rent the tough plates, but failed to reach the skin,
And Rustum plucked it back with angry groan.
Then Sohrab with his sword smote Rustum's helm,
Nor clove its steel quite through; but all the crest
He shore away, and that proud horsehair plume,
Never till now defiled, sank to the dust;
And Rustum bowed his head; but then the gloom
Grew blacker, thunder rumbled in the air,
And lightnings rent the cloud; and Ruksh, the horse,
Who stood at hand, uttered a dreadful cry;—
No horse's cry was that, most like the roar
Of some pained desert lion, who all day
Hath trailed the hunter's javelin in his side,
And comes at night to die upon the sand.
The two hosts heard that cry, and quaked for fear,
And Oxus curdled as it crossed his stream.
But Sohrab heard, and quailed not, but rushed on,
And struck again; and again Rustum bowed
His head; but this time all the blade, like glass,
Sprang in a thousand shivers on the helm,
And in his hand the hilt remained alone.
Then Rustum raised his head; his dreadful eyes
Glared, and he shook on high his menacing spear,
And shouted: *Rustum!*—Sohrab heard that shout,
And shrank amazed; back he recoiled one step
And scanned with blinking eyes the advancing form;
And then he stood bewildered; and he dropped
His covering shield, and the spear pierced his side.
He reeled, and staggering back, sank to the ground.
And then the gloom dispersed, and the wind fell,
And the bright sun broke forth, and melted all
The cloud; and the two armies saw the pair—
Saw Rustum standing, safe upon his feet,
And Sohrab, wounded, on the bloody sand.

Then, with a bitter smile, Rustum began:

"Sohrab, thou thoughtest in thy mind to kill
A Persian lord this day, and strip his corpse,
And bear thy trophies to Afrasiab's tent.
Or else that the great Rustum would come down
Himself to fight, and that thy wiles would move
His heart to take a gift, and let thee go.
And then that all the Tartar host would praise
Thy courage or thy craft, and spread thy fame,
To glad thy father in his weak old age.
Fool! thou art slain, and by an unknown man!
Dearer to the red jackals shalt thou be,
Than to thy friends, and to thy father old."
And with a fearless mien Sohrab replied:
"Unknown thou art; yet thy fierce vaunt is vain.
Thou dost not slay me, proud and boastful man!
No! Rustum slays me, and this filial heart.
For were I matched with ten such men as thee,
And I were he who till today I was,
They should be lying here, I standing there.
But that beloved name unnerved my arm—
That name, and something, I confess, in thee,
Which troubles all my heart, and made my shield
Fall; and thy spear transfixed an unarmed foe.
And now thou boastest, and insult'st my fate.
But hear thou this, fierce man, tremble to hear:
The mighty Rustum shall avenge my death!
My father, whom I seek through all the world,
He shall avenge my death, and punish thee!"

As when some hunter in the spring hath found
A breeding eagle sitting on her nest,
Upon the craggy isle of a hill-lake,
And pierced her with an arrow as she rose,
And followed her to find her where she fell
Far off;—anon her mate comes winging back
From hunting, and a great way off descries
His huddling young left sole; at that, he checks
His pinion, and with short uneasy sweeps
Circles above his eyry, with loud screams
Chiding his mate back to her nest; but she
Lies dying, with the arrow in her side,
In some far stony gorge out of his ken,
A heap of fluttering feathers—never more
Shall the lake glass her, flying over it;
Never the black and dripping precipices
Echo her stormy scream as she sails by—
As that poor bird flies home, nor knows his loss,
So Rustum knew not his own loss, but stood
Over his dying son, and knew him not.

But with a cold, incredulous voice, he said:
"What prate is this of fathers and revenge?
The mighty Rustum never had a son."

And, with a failing voice, Sohrab replied:
"Ah yes, he had! and that lost son am I.
Surely the news will one day reach his ear,
Reach Rustum, where he sits, and tarries long,
Somewhere, I know not where, but far from here;
And pierce him like a stab, and make him leap
To arms, and cry for vengeance upon thee.
Fierce man, bethink thee, for an only son!
What will that grief, what will that vengeance be!
Oh, could I live, till I that grief had seen!
Yet him I pity not so much, but her,
My mother, who in Ader-baijan dwells
With that old King, her father, who grows gray
With age, and rules over the valiant Koords.
Her most I pity, who no more will see

Sohrab returning from the Tartar camp,
With spoils and honor, when the war is done.
But a dark rumor will be bruited up,
From tribe to tribe, until it reach her ear;
And then will that defenceless woman learn
That Sohrab will rejoice her sight no more,
But that in battle with a nameless foe,
By the far distant Oxus, he is slain."

He spoke; and as he ceased he wept aloud,
Thinking of her he left, and his own death.
He spoke; but Rustum listened, plunged in thought.
Nor did he yet believe it was his son
Who spoke, although he called back names he knew;
For he had had sure tidings that the babe,
Which was in Ader-baijan born to him,
Had been a puny girl, no boy at all—
So that sad mother sent him word, for fear
Rustum should take the boy, to train in arms.
And so he deemed that either Sohrab took,
By a false boast, the style of Rustum's son;
Or that men gave it him, to swell his fame.
So deemed he; yet he listened, plunged in thought:
And his soul set to grief, as the vast tide
Of the bright rocking Ocean sets to shore
At the full moon; tears gathered in his eyes;
For he remembered his own early youth,
And all its bounding rapture; as, at dawn,
The shepherd from his mountain-lodge descries
A far bright city, smitten by the sun,
Through many rolling clouds—so Rustum saw
His youth; saw Sohrab's mother, in her bloom;
And that old King, her father, who loved well
His wandering guest, and gave him his fair child
With joy; and all the pleasant life they led,
They three, in that long-distant summer-time—
The castle, and the dewy woods, and hunt
And hound, and morn on those delightful hills
In Ader-baijan. And he saw that youth,

Of age and looks to be his own dear son,
Piteous and lovely, lying on the sand,
Like some rich hyacinth, which by the scythe
Of an unskillful gardener has been cut,
Mowing the garden grass-plots near its bed,
And lies, a fragrant tower of purple bloom,
On the mown, dying grass—so Sohrab lay,
Lovely in death, upon the common sand.
And Rustum gazed on him with grief, and said:

"O Sohrab, thou indeed art such a son
Whom Rustum, wert thou his, might well have loved!
Yet here thou errest, Sohrab, or else men
Have told thee false—thou art not Rustum's son.
For Rustum had no son; one child he had—
But one—a girl; who with her mother now
Plies some light female task, nor dreams of us—
Of us she dreams not, nor of wounds, nor war."

But Sohrab answered him in wrath; for now
The anguish of the deep-fixed spear grew fierce,
And he desired to draw forth the steel,
And let the blood flow free, and so to die—
But first he would convince his stubborn foe;
And, rising sternly on one arm, he said:

"Man, who art thou who dost deny my words?
Truth sits upon the lips of dying men,
And falsehood, while I lived, was far from mine.
I tell thee, pricked upon this arm I bear
That seal which Rustum to my mother gave,
That she might prick it on the babe she bore."

He spoke: and all the blood left Rustum's cheeks,
And his knees tottered, and he smote his hand,
Against his breast, his heavy mailed hand,
That the hard iron corslet clanked aloud;
And to his heart he pressed the other hand,
And in a hollow voice he spake, and said:

"Sohrab, that were a proof which could not lie!
If thou show this, then art thou Rustum's son."

Then, with weak hasty fingers, Sohrab loosed

His belt, and near the shoulder bared his arm,
And showed a sign in faint vermilion points
Pricked: as a cunning workman, in Pekin,
Pricks with vermilion some clear porcelain vase,
An emperor's gift—at early morn he paints,
And all day long, and, when night comes, the lamp
Lights up his studious forehead and thin hands—
So delicately pricked the sign appeared
On Sohrab's arm, the sign of Rustum's seal.
It was that griffin, which of old reared Zal,
Rustum's great father, whom they left to die,
A helpless babe, among the mountain rocks;
Him that kind creature found, and reared, and loved—
Then Rustum took it for his glorious sign.
And Sohrab bared that image on his arm,
And himself scanned it long with mournful eyes,
And then he touched it with his hand and said:

"How say'st thou? Is that sign the proper sign
Of Rustum's son, or of some other man's?"

He spoke; but Rustum gazed, and gazed, and stood
Speechless; and then he uttered one sharp cry:
O boy—thy father!—and his voice choked there.
And then a dark cloud passed before his eyes,
And his head swam, and he sank down to earth.
But Sohrab crawled to where he lay, and cast
His arms about his neck, and kissed his lips,
And with fond faltering fingers stroked his cheeks,
Trying to call him back to life; and life
Came to Rustum, and he oped his eyes,
And they stood wide with horror; and he seized
In both his hands the dust which lay around,
And threw it on his head, and smirched his hair,—
His hair, and face, and beard, and glittering arms;
And strong convulsive groanings shook his breast,
And his sobs choked him; and he clutched his sword,
To draw it, and forever let life out.
But Sohrab saw his thought, and held his hands,
And with a soothing voice he spoke, and said:

"Father, forbear: for I but meet to-day
The doom that at my birth was written down
In Heaven, and thou art Heaven's unconscious hand.
Surely my heart cried out that it was thou,
When first I saw thee; and thy heart spoke too,
I know it: but fate trod those promptings down
Under its iron heel; fate, fate engaged
The strife, and hurled me on my father's spear.
But let us speak no more of this! I find
My father; let me feel that I have found!
Come, sit beside me on this sand, and take
My head betwixt thy hands, and kiss my cheeks,
And wash them with thy tears, and say: *My Son!*
Quick! quick! for numbered are my sands of life,
And swift; for like the lightning to this field
I came, and like the wind I go away—
Sudden, and swift, and like a passing wind.
But it was writ in Heaven that this should be."

So said he, and his voice released the heart
Of Rustum, and his tears broke forth; he cast
His arms round his son's neck, and wept aloud,
And kissed him. And awe fell on both the hosts
When they saw Rustum's grief; and Ruksh, the horse,
With his head bowing to the ground, and mane
Sweeping the dust, came near, and in mute woe
First to the one then to the other moved

His head, as if inquiring what their grief
Might mean; and from his dark, compassionate eyes,
The big warm tears rolled down, and caked the sand.
But Rustum chid him with stern voice, and said:
"Ruksh, now thou grievest; but, O Ruksh, thy feet
Should then have rotted on their nimble joints,
Or ere they brought thy master to this field!"
But Sohrab looked upon the horse and said:
"Is this, then, Ruksh? How often, in past days,
My mother told me of thee, thou brave steed,
My terrible father's terrible horse! and said,
That I should one day find thy lord and thee.
Come, let me lay my hand upon thy mane!
O Ruksh, thou art more fortunate than I;
For thou hast gone where I shall never go,
And snuffed the breezes of my father's home.
And thou hast trod the sands of Seistan,
And seen the River of Helmund, and the Lake
Of Zirrah; and the aged Zal himself
Has often stroked thy neck, and given thee food,
Corn in a golden platter soaked with wine,
And said—*O Ruksh! bear Rustum well!*—but I
Have never known my grandsire's furrowed face,
Nor seen his lofty house in Seistan.
Nor slaked my thirst at the clear Helmund stream;
But lodged among my father's foes, and seen
Afrasiab's cities only, Samarcand,
Bokhara, and lone Khiva in the waste,
And the black Toorkmun tents; and only drunk
The desert rivers, Moorghab and Tejend,
Kohik, and where the Kalmuks feed their sheep,
The northern Sir; and this great Oxus stream,
The yellow Oxus, by whose brink I die."
And, with a heavy groan, Rustum bewailed:
"Oh that its waves were flowing over me!
Oh that I saw its grains of yellow silt
Roll tumbling in the current o'er my head!"
And, with a grave mild voice, Sohrab replied:

"Desire not that, my father; thou must live.
For some are born to do great deeds, and live,
As some are born to be obscured, and die.
Do thou the deeds I die too young to do,
And reap a second glory in thine age;
Thou art my father, and thy gain is mine.
But come! thou seest this great host of men
Which follow me; I pray thee, slay not these!
Let me entreat for them; what have they done?
They followed me, my hope, my fame, my star.
Let them all cross the Oxus back in peace.
But me thou must bear hence, not send with them,
But carry me with thee to Seistan,
And place me on a bed, and mourn for me,
Thou, and the snow-haired Zal, and all thy friends.
And thou must lay me in that lovely earth,
And heap a stately mound above my bones,
And plant a far-seen pillar over all.
That so the passing horseman on the waste
May see my tomb a great way off, and cry—
Sohrab, the mighty Rustum's son, lies there,
Whom his great father did in ignorance kill—
And I be not forgotten in my grave."

And, with a mournful voice, Rustum replied:
"Fear not! as thou hast said, Sohrab, my son,
So shall it be; for I will burn my tents,
And quit the host, and bear thee hence with me,
And carry thee away to Seistan,
And place thee on a bed, and mourn for thee,
With the snow-headed Zal, and all my friends.
And I will lay thee in that lovely earth,
And heap a stately mound above thy bones,
And plant a far-seen pillar over all,
And men shall not forget thee in thy grave.
And I will spare thy host; yea, let them go!
Let them all cross the Oxus back in peace!
What should I do with slaying any more?
For would that all whom I have ever slain

Might be once more alive; my bitterest foes,
And they who were called champions in their time,
And through whose death I won that fame I have—
And I were nothing but a common man,
A poor, mean soldier, and without renown,
So thou mightest live too, my son, my son!
Or rather would that I, even I myself,
Might now be lying on this bloody sand,
Near death, and by an ignorant stroke of thine,
Not thou of mine; and I might die, not thou;
And I, not thou, be borne to Seistan;
And Zal might weep above my grave, not thine;
And say—*O son, I weep thee not too sore,*
For willingly, I know, thou met'st thine end.—
But now in blood and battles was my youth,
And full of blood and battles is my age;
And I shall never end this life of blood."

Then, at the point of death, Sohrab replied:
"A life of blood indeed, thou dreadful man!
But thou shalt yet have peace; only not now;
Not yet: but thou shalt have it on that day,
When thou shalt sail in a high-masted ship,
Thou and the other peers of Kai-Khosroo,
Returning home over the salt blue sea,
From laying thy dear master in his grave."

And Rustum gazed in Sohrab's face, and said:
"Soon be that day, my Son, and deep that sea!
Till then, if fate so wills, let me endure."

He spoke; and Sohrab smiled on him, and took
The spear, and drew it from his side, and eased
His wound's imperious anguish; but the blood
Came welling from the open gash, and life
Flowed with the stream; all down his cold white side
The crimson torrent ran, dim now, and soiled,
Like the soiled tissue of white violets
Left, freshly gathered, on their native bank,
By children, whom their nurses call with haste
Indoors from the sun's eye; his head drooped low,

His limbs grew slack; motionless, white, he lay—
White, with eyes closed; only when heavy gasps,
Deep, heavy gasps, quivering through all his frame,
Convulsed him back to life, he opened them,
And fixed them feebly on his father's face;
Till now all strength was ebbed, and from his limbs
Unwillingly the spirit fled away,
Regretting the warm mansion which it left,
And youth and bloom, and this delightful world.

So, on the bloody sand, Sohrab lay dead;
And the great Rustum drew his horseman's cloak
Down o'er his face, and sate by his dead son.
As those black granite pillars, once high-reared
By Jemshid in Persepolis, to bear
His house, now, mid their broken flights of steps,
Lie prone, enormous, down the mountain side—
So in the sand lay Rustum by his son.

And night came down over the solemn waste,
And the two gazing hosts, and that sole pair,
And darkened all; and a cold fog, with night,
Crept from the Oxus. Soon a hum arose,
As of a great assembly loosed, and fires
Began to twinkle through the fog; for now
Both armies moved to camp, and took their meal;
The Persians took it on the open sands
Southward, the Tartars by the river marge;
And Rustum and his son were left alone.

But the majestic river floated on,
Out of the mist and hum of that low land,
Into the frosty starlight, and there moved,
Rejoicing, through the hushed Chorasmian waste,
Under the solitary moon: he flowed
Right for the polar star, past Orgunjé,
Brimming, and bright, and large; then sands begin
To hem his watery march, and dam his streams,
And split his currents; that for many a league
The shorn and parceled Oxus strains along
Through beds of sand and matted rushy isles—

Oxus, forgetting the bright speed he had
In his high mountain cradle in Pamere,
A foiled circuitous wanderer—till at last
The longed-for dash of waves is heard, and wide
His luminous home of waters opens, bright
And tranquil, from whose floor the new-bathed stars
Emerge, and shine upon the Aral Sea.

Christina Rossetti

GOBLIN MARKET

Morning and evening
Maids heard the goblins cry:
"Come buy our orchard fruits,
Come buy, come buy:
Apples and quinces,
Lemons and oranges,
Plump unpecked cherries,
Melons and raspberries,
Bloom-down-cheeked peaches,
Swart-headed mulberries,
Wild free-born cranberries,
Crab-apples, dewberries,
Pine-apples, blackberries,
Apricots, strawberries–
All ripe together
In summer weather–
Morns that pass by,
Fair eves that fly;
Come buy, come buy:
Our grapes fresh from the vine,
Pomegranates full and fine,
Dates and sharp bullaces,
Rare pears and greengages,
Damsons and bilberries,

Taste them and try:
Currants and gooseberries,
Bright-fire-like barberries,
Figs to fill your mouth,
Citrons from the South,
Sweet to tongue and sound to eye;
Come buy, come buy."

Evening by evening
Among the brookside rushes,
Laura bowed her head to hear,
Lizzie veiled her blushes:
Crouching close together
In the cooling weather,
With clasping arms and cautioning lips,
With tingling cheeks and finger tips.
"Lie close," Laura said,
Pricking up her golden head:
"We must not look at goblin men,
We must not buy their fruits:
Who knows upon what soil they fed
Their hungry thirsty roots?"
"Come buy," call the goblins
Hobbling down the glen.
"Oh," cried Lizzie, "Laura, Laura,
You should not peep at goblin men."
Lizzie covered up her eyes,
Covered close lest they should look;
Laura reared her glossy head,
And whispered like the restless brook:
"Look, Lizzie, look, Lizzie,
Down the glen tramp little men.
One hauls a basket,
One bears a plate,
One lugs a golden dish
Of many pounds weight.
How fair the vine must grow
Whose grapes are so luscious;

How warm the wind must blow
Through those fruit bushes."
"No," said Lizzie: "No, no, no;
Their offers should not charm us,
Their evil gifts would harm us."
She thrust a dimpled finger
In each ear, shut eyes and ran:
Curious Laura chose to linger
Wondering at each merchant man.
One had a cat's face,
One whisked a tail,
One tramped at a rat's pace,
One crawled like a snail,
One like a wombat prowled obtuse and furry,
One like a ratel tumbled hurry skurry.
She heard a voice like voice of doves
Cooing all together:
They sounded kind and full of loves
In the pleasant weather.

Laura stretched her gleaming neck
Like a rush-imbedded swan,
Like a lily from the beck,
Like a moonlit poplar branch,
Like a vessel at the launch
When its last restraint is gone.

Backwards up the mossy glen
Turned and trooped the goblin men.
With their shrill repeated cry,
"Come buy, come buy."
When they reached where Laura was
They stood stock still upon the moss,
Leering at each other,
Brother with queer brother;
Signaling each other,
Brother with sly brother.
One set his basket down,

One reared his plate;
One began to weave a crown
Of tendrils, leaves, and rought nuts brown
(Men sell not such in any town);
One heaved the golden weight
Of dish and fruit to offer her:
"Come buy, come buy," was still their cry.
Laura stared but did not stir,
Longed but had no money:
The whisk-tailed merchant bade her taste
In tones as smooth as honey,
The cat-faced purr'd,
The rat-paced spoke a word
Of welcome, and the snail-paced even was heard;
One parrot-voiced and jolly
Cried "Pretty Goblin" still for "Pretty Polly;"–
One whistled like a bird.

But sweet-tooth Laura spoke in haste:
"Good folk, I have no coin;
To take were to purloin:
I have no copper in my purse,
I have no silver either,
And all my gold is on the furze
That shakes in windy weather
Above the rusty heather."
"You have much gold upon your head,"
They answered all together:
"Buy from us with a golden curl."
She clipped a precious golden lock,
She dropped a tear more rare than pearl,
Then sucked their fruit globes fair or red:
Sweeter than honey from the rock,

Stronger than man-rejoicing wine,
Clearer than water flowed that juice;
She never tasted such before,
How should it cloy with length of use?
She sucked and sucked and sucked the more
Fruits which that unknown orchard bore;
She sucked until her lips were sore;
Then flung the emptied rinds away
But gathered up one kernel stone,
And knew not was it night or day
As she turned home alone.

Lizzie met her at the gate
Full of wise upbraidings:
"Dear, you should not stay so late,
Twilight is not good for maidens;
Should not loiter in the glen
In the haunts of goblin men.
Do you not remember Jeanie,
How she met them in the moonlight,
Took their gifts both choice and many,
Ate their fruits and wore their flowers
Plucked from bowers
Where summer ripens at all hours?
But ever in the noonlight
She pined and pined away;
Sought them by night and day,
Found them no more but dwindled and grew gray;
Then fell with the first snow,
While to this day no grass will grow
Where she lies low:
I planted daisies there a year ago
That never blow.
You should not loiter so."
"Nay, hush," said Laura:
"Nay, hush, my sister:
I ate and ate my fill,
Yet my mouth waters still;

To-morrow night I will
Buy more:" and kissed her:
"Have done with sorrow;
I'll bring you plums to-morrow
Fresh on their mother twigs,
Cherries worth getting;
You cannot think what figs
My teeth have met in,
What melons icy-cold
Piled on a dish of gold
Too huge for me to hold,
What peaches with a velvet nap,
Pellucid grapes without one seed:
Odorous indeed must be the mead
Whereon they grow, and pure the wave they drink
With lilies at the brink,
And sugar-sweet their sap."

Golden head by golden head,
Like two pigeons in one nest
Folded in each other's wings,
They lay down in their curtained bed:
Like two blossoms on one stem,
Like two flakes of new-fall'n snow,
Like two wands of ivory
Tipped with gold for awful kings.
Moon and stars gazed in at them,
Wind sang to them lullaby,
Lumbering owls forbore to fly,
Not a bat flapped to and fro
Round their nest:
Cheek to cheek and breast to breast
Locked together in one nest.

Early in the morning
When the first cock crowed his warning,
Neat like bees, as sweet and busy,
Laura rose with Lizzie:

Fetched in honey, milked the cows,
Aired and set to rights the house,
Kneaded cakes of whitest wheat,
Cakes for dainty mouths to eat,
Next churned butter, whipped up cream,
Fed their poultry, sat and sewed;
Talked as modest maidens should:
Lizzie with an open heart,
Laura in an absent dream,
One content, one sick in part;
One warbling for the mere bright day's delight,
One longing for the night.

At length slow evening came;
They went with pitchers to the reedy brook;
Lizzie most placid in her look,
Laura most like a leaping flame.
They drew the gurgling water from its deep;
Lizzie plucked purple and rich golden flags,
Then turning homewards said: "The sunset flushes
Those furthest loftiest crags;
Come, Laura, not another maiden lags,
No wilful squirrel wags,
The beasts and birds are fast asleep."
But Laura loitered still among the rushes
And said the bank was steep.

And said the hour was early still,
The dew not fall'n, the wind not chill:
Listening ever, but not catching
The customary cry,
"Come buy, come buy,"
With its iterated jingle
Of sugar-baited words:
Not for all her watching
Once discerning even one goblin
Racing, whisking, tumbling, hobbling;
Let alone the herds

That used to tramp along the glen,
In groups or single,
Of brisk fruit-merchant men.

Till Lizzie urged, "O Laura, come;
I hear the fruit-call but I dare not look:
You should not loiter longer at this brook:
Come with me home.
The stars rise, the moon bends her arc,
Each glowworm winks her spark,
Let us get home before the night grows dark:
For clouds may gather
Though this is summer weather,
Put out the lights and drench us through;
Then if we lost our way what should we do?"

Laura turned cold as stone
To find her sister heard that cry alone,
That goblin cry,
"Come buy our fruits, come buy."
Must she then buy no more such dainty fruit?
Must she no more such succous pasture find,
Gone deaf and blind?
Her tree of life drooped from the root:
She said not one word in her heart's sore ache;
But peering thro' the dimness, nought discerning,
Trudged home, her pitcher dripping all the way;
So crept to bed, and lay
Silent till Lizzie slept;
Then sat up in a passionate yearning,
And gnashed her teeth for balked desire, and wept
As if her heart would break.

Day after day, night after night,
Laura kept watch in vain
In sullen silence of exceeding pain.
She never caught again the goblin cry:
"Come buy, come buy;"—

She never spied the goblin men
Hawking their fruits along the glen:
But when the moon waxed bright
Her hair grew thin and gray;
She dwindled, as the fair full moon doth turn
To swift decay and burn
Her fire away.

One day remembering her kernel-stone
She set it by a wall that faced the south;
Dewed it with tears, hoped for a root,
Watched for a waxing shoot,
But there came none;
It never saw the sun,
It never felt the trickling moisture run:
While with sunk eyes and faded mouth
She dreamed of melons, as a traveler sees
False waves in desert drouth
With shade of leaf-crowned trees,
And burns the thirstier in the sandful breeze.

She no more swept the house,
Tended the fowls or cows,
Fetched honey, kneaded cakes of wheat,
Brought water from the brook,
But sat down listless in the chimney-nook
And would not eat.

Tender Lizzie could not bear
To watch her sister's cankerous care
Yet not to share.
She night and morning
Caught the goblins' cry:

"Come buy our orchard fruits,
Come buy, come buy;"–
Beside the brook, along the glen,
She heard the tramp of goblin men,
The voice and stir
Poor Laura could not hear;
Longed to buy fruit to comfort her
But feared to pay too dear.
She thought of Jeanie in her grave,
Who should have been a bride;
But who for joys brides hope to have
Fell sick and died
In her gay prime,
In earliest Winter time,
With the first glazing rime,
With the first snow-fall of crisp Winter time.

Till Laura dwindling
Seemed knocking at Death's door:
Then Lizzie weighed no more
Better and worse;
But put a silver penny in her purse,
Kissed Laura, crossed the heath with clumps of furze
At twilight, halted by the brook:
And for the first time in her life
Began to listen and look.

Laughed every goblin
When they spied her peeping:
Came towards her hobbling,
Flying, running, leaping,
Puffing and blowing,
Chuckling, clapping, crowing,
Clucking and gobbling,
Mopping and mowing,
Full of airs and graces,
Pulling wry faces,
Demure grimaces,

Cat-like and rat-like,
Ratel- and wombat-like,
Snail-paced in a hurry,
Parrot-voiced and whistler,
Helter skelter, hurry skurry,
Chattering like magpies,
Fluttering like pigeons,
Gliding like fishes,—
Hugged her and kissed her:
Squeezed and caressed her:
Stretched up their dishes,
Panniers, and plates:
"Look at our apples
Russet and dun,
Bob at our cherries,
Bite at our peaches,
Citrons and dates,
Grapes for the asking,
Pears red with basking
Out in the sun,
Plums on their twigs;
Pluck them and suck them,
Pomegranates, figs."—

"Good folk," said Lizzie,
Mindful of Jeanie:
"Give me much and many:"—
Held out her apron,
Tossed them her penny.
"Nay, take a seat with us,
Honor and eat with us,"
They answered grinning:
"Our feast is but beginning.
Night yet is early,
Warm and dew-pearly,
Wakeful and starry:
Such fruits as these
No man can carry;

Half their bloom would fly,
Half their dew would dry,
Half their flavor would pass by.
Sit down and feast with us,
Be welcome guest with us,
Cheer you, and rest with us."—
"Thank you," said Lizzie: "But one waits
At home alone for me:
So without further parleying,
If you will not sell me any
Of your fruits though much and many,
Give me back my silver penny
I tossed you for a fee."—
They began to scratch their pates,
No longer wagging, purring,
But visibly demurring,
Grunting and snarling.
One called her proud,
Cross-grained, uncivil;
Their tones waxed loud,
Their looks were evil.
Lashing their tails
They trod and hustled her,
Elbowed and jostled her,
Clawed with their nails,
Barking, mewing, hissing, mocking,
Tore her gown and soiled her stocking,
Twitched her hair out by the roots,
Stamped upon her tender feet,
Held her hands and squeezed their fruits
Against her mouth to make her eat.

White and golden Lizzie stood,
Like a lily in a flood,—
Like a rock of blue-veined stone
Lashed by tides obstreperously,—
Like a beacon left alone
In a hoary roaring sea,

Sending up a golden fire,–
Like a fruit-crowned orange-tree
White with blossoms honey-sweet
Sore beset by wasp and bee,–
Like a royal virgin town
Topped with gilded dome and spire
Close beleaguered by a fleet
Mad to tug her standard down.

One may lead a horse to water,
Twenty cannot make him drink.
Though the goblins cuffed and caught her,
Coaxed and fought her,
Bullied and besought her,
Scratched her, pinched her black as ink,
Kicked and knocked her,
Mauled and mocked her,
Lizzie uttered not a word;
Would not open lip from lip
Lest they should cram a mouthful in:
But laughed in heart to feel the drip
Of juice that syrupped all her face,
And lodged in dimples of her chin,
And streaked her neck which quaked like curd.
At last the evil people
Worn out by her resistance
Flung back her penny, kicked their fruit
Along whichever road they took,
Not leaving root or stone or shoot;
Some writhed into the ground,
Some dived into the brook
With ring and ripple,
Some scudded on the gale without a sound,
Some vanished in the distance.

In a smart, ache, tingle,
Lizzie went her way;
Knew not was it night or day;

Sprang up the bank, tore thro' the furze,
Threaded copse and dingle,
And heard her penny jingle
Bouncing in her purse,—
Its bounce was music to her ear.
She ran and ran
As if she feared some goblin man
Dogged her with gibe or curse
Of something worse:
But not one goblin skurried after,
Nor was she pricked by fear;
The kind heart made her windy-paced
That urged her home quite out of breath with haste
And inward laughter.

She cried "Laura," up the garden,
"Did you miss me?
Come and kiss me.
Never mind my bruises,
Hug me, kiss me, suck my juices
Squeezed from goblin fruits for you,
Goblin pulp and goblin dew.
Eat me, drink me, love me;
Laura, make much of me:
For your sake I have braved the glen
And had to do with goblin merchant men."

Laura started from her chair,
Flung her arms up in the air,
Clutched her hair:
"Lizzie, Lizzie, have you tasted
For my sake the fruit forbidden?
Must your light like mine be hidden,

Your young life like mine be wasted,
Undone in mine undoing
And ruined in my ruin,
Thirsty, cankered, goblin-ridden?"—
She clung about her sister,
Kissed and kissed and kissed her:
Tears once again
Refreshed her shrunken eyes,
Dropping like rain
After long sultry drouth;
Shaking with aguish fear, and pain,
She kissed and kissed her with a hungry mouth.

Her lips began to scorch,
That juice was wormwood to her tongue,
She loathed the feast:
Writhing as one possessed she leaped and sung,
Rent all her robe, and wrung
Her hands in lamentable haste,
And beat her breast.
Her locks streamed like the torch
Borne by a racer at full speed,
Or like the mane of horses in their flight,
Or like an eagle when she stems the light
Straight toward the sun,
Or like a caged thing freed,
Or like a flying flag when armies run.

Swift fire spread through her veins, knocked at her heart,
Met the fire smoldering there
And overbore its lesser flame;
She gorged on bitterness without a name:
Ah! fool, to choose such part
Of soul-consuming care!
Sense failed in the mortal strife:
Like the watch-tower of a town
Which an earthquake shatters down,
Like a lightning-stricken mast,

Like a wind-uprooted tree
Spun about,
Like a foam-topped waterspout
Cast down headlong in the sea,
She fell at last;
Pleasure past and anguish past,
Is it death or is it life?

Life out of death
That night long Lizzie watched by her,
Counted her pulse's flagging stir,
Felt for her breath,
Held water to her lips, and cooled her face
With tears and fanning leaves:
But when the first birds chirped about their eaves,
And early reapers plodded to the place
Of golden sheaves,
And dew-wet grass
Bowed in the morning winds so brisk to pass,
And new buds with new day
Opened of cup-like lilies on the stream,
Laura awoke as from a dream,
Laughed in the innocent old way,
Hugged Lizzie but not twice or thrice;
Her gleaming locks showed not one thread of grey,
Her breath was sweet as May
And light danced in her eyes.

Days, weeks, months, years
Afterwards, when both were wives
With children of their own
Their mother-hearts beset with fears,
Their lives bound up in tender lives;
Laura would call the little ones
And tell them of her early prime,
Those pleasant days long gone
Of not-returning time:
Would talk about the haunted glen,

The wicked, quaint fruit-merchant men,
Their fruits like honey to the throat
But poisons in the blood;
(Men sell not such in any town:)
Would tell them how her sister stood
In deadly peril to do her good,
And win the fiery antidote:
Then joining hands to little hands
Would bid them cling together,
"For there is no friend like a sister
In calm or stormy weather;
To cheer one on the tedious way,
To fetch one if one goes astray,
To lift one if one totters down,
To strengthen whilst one stands."

ATALANTA'S RACE

Through thick Arcadian woods a hunter went,
Following the beasts up, on a fresh spring day;
But since his horn-tipped bow but seldom bent,
Now at the noontide nought had happed to slay,
Within a vale he called his hounds away,
Hearkening the echoes of his lone voice cling
About the cliffs and through the beech-trees ring.

But when they ended, still awhile he stood,
And but the sweet familiar thrush could hear,
And all the day-long noises of the wood,
And o'er the dry leaves of the vanished year
His hound's feet pattering as they drew anear,
And heavy breathing from their heads low hung,
To see the mighty cornel bow unstrung.

Then smiling did he turn to leave the place,
But with his first step some new fleeting thought
A shadow cast across his sun-burnt face;
I think the golden net that April brought
From some warm world his wavering soul had caught;
For, sunk in vague sweet longing, did he go
Betwixt the trees with doubtful steps and slow.

Yet howsoever slow he went, at last
The trees grew sparser, and the wood was done;
Whereon one farewell, backward look he cast,
Then, turning round to see what place was won,
With shaded eyes looked underneath the sun,
And o'er green meads and new-turned furrows brown
Beheld the gleaming of King Schoeneus' town.

So thitherward he turned, and on each side
The folk were busy on the teeming land,
And man and maid from the brown furrows cried,
Or midst the newly-blossomed vines did stand,
And as the rustic weapon pressed the hand
Thought of the nodding of the well-filled ear,
Or how the knife the heavy bunch should shear.

Merry it was: about him sung the birds,
The spring flowers bloomed along the firm dry road,
The sleek-skinned mothers of the sharp-horned herds
Now for the barefoot milking-maidens lowed;
While from the freshness of his blue abode,
Glad his death-bearing arrows to forget,
The broad sun blazed, nor scattered plagues as yet.

Through such fair things unto the gates he came,
And found them open, as though peace were there;
Wherethrough, unquestioned of his race or name,
He entered, and along the streets 'gan fare,
Which at the first of folk were well-nigh bare;
But pressing on, and going more hastily,
Men hurrying too he 'gan at last to see.

Following the last of these, he still pressed on,
Until an open space he came unto,
Where wreaths of fame had oft been lost and won,
For feats of strength folk there were wont to do.
And now our hunter looked for something new,
Because the whole wide space was bare, and stilled
The high seats were, with eager people filled.

There with the others to a seat he gat,
Whence he beheld a broidered canopy,
'Neath which in fair array King Schoeneus sat
Upon his throne with councilors thereby;
And underneath his well-wrought seat and high,
He saw a golden image of the sun,
A silver image of the Fleet-foot One.

A brazen altar stood beneath their feet
Whereon a thin flame flickered in the wind;
Nigh this a herald clad in raiment meet
Made ready even now his horn to wind,
By whom a huge man held a sword, entwined
With yellow flowers; these stood a little space
From off the altar, nigh the starting place.

And there two runners did the sign abide
Foot set to foot,–a young man slim and fair,
Crisp-haired, well knit, with firm limbs often tried
In places where no man his strength may spare;
Dainty his thin coat was, and on his hair
A golden circlet of renown he wore,
And in his hand an olive garland bore.

But on this day with whom shall he contend?
A maid stood by him like Diana clad
When in the wood she lists her bow to bend,
Too fair for one to look on and be glad,
Who scarcely yet has thirty summers had,
If he must still behold her from afar;
Too fair to let the world live free from war.

She seemed all earthly matters to forget;
Of all tormenting lines her face was clear.
Her wide gray eyes upon the goal were set
Calm and unmoved as though no soul were near,
But her foe trembled as a man in fear,
Nor from her loveliness one moment turned
His anxious face with fierce desire that burned.

Now through the hush there broke the trumpet's clang
Just as the setting sun made eventide.
Then from light feet a spurt of dust there sprang,
And swiftly were they running side by side;
But silent did the thronging folk abide
Until the turning-post was reached at last,
And round about it still abreast they passed.

But when the people saw how close they ran,
When halfway to the starting-point they were,
A cry of joy broke forth, whereat the man
Headed the white-foot runner, and drew near
Unto the very end of all his fear;
And scarce his straining feet the ground could feel,
And bliss unhoped for o'er his heart 'gan steal.

But midst the loud victorious shouts he heard
Her footsteps drawing nearer, and the sound
Of fluttering raiment, and thereat afeard
His flushed and eager face he turned around,
And even then he felt her past him bound
Fleet as the wind, but scarcely saw her there
Till on the goal she laid her fingers fair.

There stood she breathing like a little child
Amid some warlike clamor laid asleep,
For no victorious joy her red lips smiled,
Her cheek its wonted freshness did but keep;
No glance lit up her clear grey eyes and deep,
Though some divine thought softened all her face
As once more rang the trumpet through the place.

But her late foe stopped short amidst his course,
One moment gazed upon her piteously,
Then with the groan his lingering feet did force
To leave the spot whence he her eyes could see;
And, changed like one who knows his time must be
But short and bitter, without any word
He knelt before the bearer of the sword;

Then high rose up the gleaming deadly blade,
Bared of its flowers, and through the crowded place
Was silence now, and midst of it the maid
Went by the poor wretch at a gentle pace,
And he to hers upturned his sad white face:
Nor did his eyes behold another sight
Ere on his soul there fell eternal night.

So was the pageant ended, and all folk
Talking of this and that familiar thing
In little groups from that sad concourse broke,
For now the shrill bats were upon the wing,
And soon dark night would slay the evening,
And in dark gardens sang the nightingale
Her little-heeded, oft-repeated tale.

And with the last of all the hunter went,
Who, wondering at the strange sight he had seen,
Prayed an old man to tell him what it meant,
Both why the vanquished man so slain had been,
And if the maiden were an earthly queen,
Or rather what much more she seemed to be,
No sharer in the world's mortality.

"Stranger," said he, "I pray she soon may die
Whose lovely youth has slain so many an one!
King Schoeneus' daughter is she verily,
Who when her eyes first looked upon the sun

Was fain to end her life but new begun,
For he had vowed to leave but men alone
Sprung from his loins when he from earth was gone.

"Therefore he bade one leave her in the wood,
And let wild things deal with her as they might,
But this being done, some cruel god thought good
To save her beauty in the world's despite:
Folk say that her, so delicate and white
As now she is, a rough root-grubbing bear
Amidst her shapeless cubs at first did rear.

"In course of time the woodfolk slew her nurse,
And to their rude abode the youngling brought,
And reared her up to be a kingdom's curse,
Who grown a woman, of no kingdom thought,
But armed and swift, 'mid beasts destruction wrought,
Nor spared two shaggy centaur kings to slay
To whom her body seemed an easy prey.

"So to this city, led by fate, she came
Whom known by signs, whereof I cannot tell,
King Schoeneus for his child at last did claim.
Nor otherwhere since that day doth she dwell
Sending too many a noble soul to hell—
What! thine eyes glisten! what then, thinkest thou
Her shining head unto the yoke to bow?

"Listen, my son, and love some other maid,
For she the saffron gown will never wear,
And on no flower-strewn couch shall she be laid,
Nor shall her voice make glad a lover's ear:
Yet if of Death thou hast not any fear,
Yea, rather, if thou lovest him utterly,
Thou still may'st woo her ere thou com'st to die,

"Like him that on this day thou sawest lie dead;
For, fearing as I deem the sea-born one,
The maid has vowed e'en such a man to wed

As in the course her swift feet can outrun,
But whoso fails herein, his days are done:
He came the nighest that was slain to-day,
Although with him I deem she did but play.

"Behold, such mercy Atalanta gives
To those that long to win her loveliness;
Be wise! Be sure that many a maid there lives
Gentler than she, of beauty little less,
Whose swimming eyes thy loving words shall bless,
When in some garden, knee set close to knee,
Thou sing'st the song that love may teach to thee."

So to the hunter spake that ancient man,
And left him for his own home presently:
But he turned round, and through the moonlight wan
Reached the thick wood, and there 'twixt tree and tree
Distraught he passed the long night feverishly,
'Twixt sleep and waking, and at dawn arose
To wage hot war against his speechless foes.

There to the hart's flank seemed his shaft to grow
As panting down the broad green glades he flew,
There by his horn the Dryads well might know
His thrust against the bear's heart had been true,
And there Adonis' bane his javelin slew,
But still in vain through rough and smooth he went
For none the more his restlessness was spent.

So wandering, he to Argive cities came,
And in the lists with valiant men he stood,
And by great deeds he won him praise and fame,
And heaps of wealth for little-valued blood;
But none of all these things, or life, seemed good
Unto his heart, where still unsatisfied
A ravenous longing warred with fear and pride.

Therefore it happed when but a month had gone
Since he had left King Schoeneus' city old,
In hunting-gear again, again alone
The forest-bordered meads did he behold,
Where still mid thoughts of August's quivering gold
Folk hoed the wheat, and clipped the vine in trust
Of faint October's purple-foaming must.

And once again he passed the peaceful gate,
While to his beating heart his lips did lie,
That owning not victorious love and fate,
Said, half aloud, "And here too must I try,
To win of alien men the mastery,
And gather for my head fresh meed of fame
And cast new glory on my father's name."

In spite of that, how beat his heart when first
Folk said to him, "And art thou come to see
That which still makes our city's name accurst
Among all mothers for its cruelty?
Then know indeed that fate is good to thee
Because to-morrow a new luckless one
Against the whitefoot maid is pledged to run."

So on the morrow with no curious eyes
As once he did, that piteous sight he saw,
Nor did that wonder in his heart arise
As toward the goal the conquering maid 'gan draw,
Nor did he gaze upon her eyes with awe,
Too full the pain of longing filled his heart
For fear or wonder there to have a part.

But, O, how long the night was ere it went!
How long it was before the dawn begun
Showed to the wakening birds the sun's intent
That not in darkness should the world be done!
And then, and then, how long before the sun
Bade silently the toilers of the earth
Get forth to fruitless cares or empty mirth!

And long it seemed that in the market-place
He stood and saw the chaffering folk go by,
Ere from the ivory throne King Schoeneus' face
Looked down upon the murmur royally,
But then came trembling that the time was nigh
When he midst pitying looks his love must claim,
And jeering voices must salute his name.

But as the throng he pierced to gain the throne,
His alien face distraught and anxious told
What hopeless errand he was bound upon,
And, each to each, folk whispered to behold
His godlike limbs; nay, and one woman old
As he went by must pluck him by the sleeve
And pray him yet that wretched love to leave.

For sidling up she said, "Canst thou live twice,
Fair son? canst thou have joyful youth again,
That thus thou goest to the sacrifice
Thyself the victim? Nay then, all in vain
Thy mother bore her longing and her pain
And one more maiden on the earth must dwell
Hopeless of joy, nor fearing death and hell.

"O, fool, thou knowest not the compact then
That with the threeformed goddess she has made
To keep her from the loving lips of men,
And in no saffron gown to be arrayed,

And therewithal with glory to be paid,
And love of her the moonlit river sees
White 'gainst the shadow of the formless trees.

"Come back, and I myself will pray for thee
Unto the sea-born framer of delights,
To give thee her who on the earth may be
The fairest stirrer up to death and fights,
To quench with hopeful days and joyous nights
The flame that doth thy youthful heart consume:
Come back, nor give thy beauty to the tomb."

How should he listen to her earnest speech?
Words, such as he not once or twice had said
Unto himself, whose meaning scarce could reach
The firm abode of that sad hardihead—
He turned about, and through the marketstead
Swiftly he passed, until before the throne
In the cleared space he stood at last alone.

Then said the King, "Stranger, what dost thou here?
Have any of my folk done ill to thee?
Or art thou of the forest men in fear?
Or art thou of the sad fraternity
Who still will strive my daughter's mates to be,
Staking their lives to win to earthly bliss
The lonely maid, the friend of Artemis?"

"O King," he said, "thou sayest the word indeed;
Nor will I quit the strife till I have won
My sweet delight, or death to end my need.
And know that I am called Milanion,
Of King Amphidamas the well-loved son:
So fear not that to thy old name, O King,
Much loss or shame my victory will bring."

"Nay, Prince," said Schoeneus, "welcome to this land
Thou wert indeed, if thou wert here to try
Thy strength 'gainst some one mighty of his hand;

Nor would we grudge thee well-won mastery.
But now, why wilt thou come to me to die,
And at my door lay down thy luckless head,
Swelling the band of the unhappy dead,

"Whose curses even now my heart doth fear?
Lo, I am old, and know what life can be,
And what a bitter thing is death anear.
O Son! be wise, and hearken unto me,
And if no other can be dear to thee,
At least as now, yet is the world full wide,
And bliss in seeming hopeless hearts may hide:

"But if thou losest life, then all is lost."
"Nay, King," Milanion said, "thy words are vain.
Doubt not that I have counted well the cost.
But say, on what day wilt thou that I gain
Fulfilled delight, or death to end my pain?
Right glad were I if it could be to-day,
And all my doubts at rest for ever lay."

"Nay," said King Schoeneus, "thus it shall not be,
But rather shalt thou let a month go by,
And weary with thy prayers for victory
What god thou know'st the kindest and most nigh.
So doing, still perchance thou shalt not die:
And with my goodwill wouldst thou have the maid,
For of the equal gods I grow afraid.

"And until then, O Prince, be thou my guest,
And all these troublous things awhile forget."
"Nay," said he, "couldst thou give my soul good rest,
And on mine head a sleepy garland set,
Then had I 'scaped the meshes of the net,
Nor shouldst thou hear from me another word;
But now, make sharp thy fearful heading sword.

"Yet will I do what son of man may do,
And promise all the gods may most desire,
That to myself I may at least be true;
And on that day my heart and limbs so tire,
With utmost strain and measureless desire,
That, at the worst, I may but fall asleep
When in the sunlight round that sword shall sweep."

He went with that, nor anywhere would bide,
But unto Argos restlessly did wend;
And there, as one who lays all hope aside,
Because the leech has said his life must end,
Silent farewell he bade to foe and friend,
And took his way unto the restless sea,
For there he deemed his rest and help might be.

Upon the shore of Argolis there stands
A temple to the goddess that he sought,
That, turned unto the lion-bearing lands,
Fenced from the east, of cold winds hath no thought,
Though to no homestead there the sheaves are brought,
No groaning press torments the close-clipped murk,
Lonely the fane stands, far from all men's work.

Pass through a close, set thick with myrtle-trees,
Through the brass doors that guard the holy place,
And entering, hear the washing of the seas
That twice a day rise high above the base,
And with the south-west urging them, embrace
The marble feet of her that standeth there
That shrink not, naked though they be and fair.

Small is the fane through which the seawind sings
About Queen Venus' well-wrought image white,
But hung around are many precious things,
The gifts of those who, longing for delight,
Have hung them there within the goddess' sight,
And in return have taken at her hands
The living treasures of the Grecian lands.

And thither now has come Milanion,
And showed unto the priests' wide open eyes
Gifts fairer than all those that there have shone,
Silk cloths, inwrought with Indian fantasies,
And bowls inscribed with sayings of the wise
Above the deeds of foolish living things,
And mirrors fit to be the gifts of kings.

And now before the Sea-born One he stands,
By the sweet veiling smoke made dim and soft,
And while the incense trickles from his hands,
And while the odorous smoke-wreaths hang aloft,
Thus doth he pray to her: "O Thou, who oft
Hast holpen man and maid in their distress,
Despise me not for this my wretchedness!

"O goddess, among us who dwell below,
Kings and great men, great for a little while,
Have pity on the lowly heads that bow,
Nor hate the hearts that love them without guile;
Wilt thou be worse than these, and is thy smile
A vain device of him who set thee here,
An empty dream of some artificer?

"O, great one, some men love, and are ashamed,
Some men are weary of the bonds of love;
Yea, and by some men lightly art thou blamed,
That from thy toils their lives they cannot move,
And 'mid the ranks of men their manhood prove.
Alas! O goddess, if thou slayest me
What new immortal can I serve but thee?

"Think then, will it bring honor to thy head
If folk say, 'Everything aside he cast
And to all fame and honor was he dead,
And to his one hope now is dead at last,
Since all unholpen he is gone and past:
Ah, the gods love not man, for certainly,
He to his helper did not cease to cry.'

"Nay, but thou wilt help; they who died before
Not single-hearted as I deem came here,
Therefore unthanked they had their gifts before
Thy stainless feet, still shivering with their fear,
Lest in their eyes their true thought might appear,
Who sought to be the lords of that fair town,
Dreaded of men and winners of renown.

"O Queen, thou knowest I pray not for this:
O set us down together in some place
Where not a voice can break our heaven of bliss,
Where nought but rocks and I can see her face,
Softening beneath the marvel of thy grace,
Where not a foot our vanished steps can track—
The golden age, the golden age come back!

"O fairest, hear me now who do thy will,
Plead for they rebel that he be not slain,
But live and love and be thy servant still;
Ah, give her joy and take away my pain,
And thus two long-enduring servants gain.
An easy thing this is to do for me,
What need of my vain words to weary thee!

"But none the less, this place will I not leave
Until I needs must go my death to meet,
Or at thy hands some happy sign receive
That in great joy we twain may one day greet

Thy presence here and kiss thy silver feet,
Such as we deem thee, fair beyond all words,
Victorious o'er our servants and our lords."

Then from the altar back a space he drew,
But from the Queen turned not his face away,
But 'gainst a pillar leaned, until the blue
That arched the sky, at ending of the day,
Was turned to ruddy gold and changing gray,
And clear, but low, the nigh-ebbed windless sea
In the still evening murmured ceaselessly.

And there he stood when all the sun was down,
Nor had he moved when the dim golden light,
Like a far lustre of a godlike town,
Had left the world to seeming hopeless night,
Nor would he move the more when wan moonlight
Streamed through the pillars for a little while,
And lighted up the white Queen's changeless smile.

Nought noted he the shallow flowing sea
As step by step it set the wrack a-swim,
The yellow torchlight nothing noted he
Wherein with fluttering gown and half-bared limb
The temple damsels sung their midnight hymn,
And nought the doubled stillness of the fane
When they were gone and all was hushed again.

But when the waves had touched the marble base,
And steps the fish swim over twice a-day,
The dawn beheld him sunken in his place
Upon the floor; and sleeping there he lay,
Not heeding aught the little jets of spray
The roughened sea brought nigh, across him cast,
For as one dead all thought from him had passed.

Yet long before the sun had showed his head,
Long ere the varied hangings on the wall
Had gained once more their blue and green and red,

He rose as one some well-known sign doth call
When war upon the city's gates doth fall,
And scarce like one fresh risen out of sleep,
He 'gan again his broken watch to keep.

Then he turned round; not for the sea-gull's cry
That wheeled above the temple in his flight,
Not for the fresh south wind that lovingly
Breathed on the new-born day and dying night,
But some strange hope 'twixt fear and great delight
Drew round his face, now flushed, now pale and wan,
And still constrained his eyes the sea to scan.

Now a faint light lit up the southern sky,
Not sun or moon, for all the world was gray,
But this a bright cloud seemed, that drew anigh,
Lighting the dull waves that beneath it lay
As toward the temple still it took its way,
And still grew greater, till Milanion
Saw nought for dazzling light that round him shone.

But as he staggered with his arms outspread,
Delicious unnamed odors breathed around.
For languid happiness he bowed his head,
And with wet eyes sank down upon the ground,
Nor wished for aught, nor any dream he found
To give him reason for that happiness,
Or make him ask more knowledge of his bliss.

At last his eyes were cleared, and he could see
Through happy tears the goddess face to face
With that faint image of Divinity,
Whose well-wrought smile and dainty changeless grace
Until that morn so gladdened all the place;
Then he unwitting cried aloud her name
And covered up his eyes for fear and shame.

But through the stillness he her voice could hear
Piercing his heart with joy scarce bearable,
That said, "Milanion, wherefore dost thou fear,
I am not hard to those who love me well;
List to what I a second time will tell,
And thou mayest hear perchance, and live to save
The cruel maiden from a loveless grave.

"See, by my feet three golden apples lie—
Such fruit among the heavy roses falls,
Such fruit my watchful damsels carefully
Store up within the best loved of my walls,
Ancient Damascus, where the lover calls,
Above my unseen head, and faint and light
The rose-leaves flutter round me in the night.

"And note, that these are not alone most fair
With heavenly gold, but longing strange they bring
Unto the hearts of men, who will not care,
Beholding these, for any once-loved thing
Till round the shining sides their fingers cling.
And thou shalt see thy well-girt swiftfoot maid
By sight of these amid her glory stayed.

"For bearing these within a scrip with thee,
When first she heads thee from the starting-place
Cast down the first one for her eyes to see,
And when she turns aside make on apace,
And if again she heads thee in the race
Spare not the other two to cast aside
If she not long enough behind will bide.

"Farewell, and when has come the happy time
That she Diana's raiment must unbind
And all the world seems blessed with Saturn's clime,
And thou with eager arms about her twined
Beholdest first her gray eyes growing kind,
Surely, O trembler, thou shalt scarcely then
Forget the Helper of unhappy men."

Milanion raised his head at this last word,
For now so soft and kind she seemed to be
No longer of her Godhead was he feared;
Too late he looked, for nothing could he see
But the white image glimmering doubtfully
In the departing twilight cold and gray,
And those three apples on the steps that lay.

These then he caught up quivering with delight,
Yet fearful lest it all might be a dream,
And though aweary with the watchful night,
And sleepless nights of longing, still did deem
He could not sleep; but yet the first sunbeam
That smote the fane across the heaving deep
Shone on him laid in calm untroubled sleep.

But little ere the noontide did he rise,
And why he felt so happy scarce could tell
Until the gleaming apples met his eyes.
Then leaving the fair place where this befell
Oft he looked back as one who loved it well,
Then homeward to the haunts of men 'gan wend
To bring all things unto a happy end.

Now has the lingering month at last gone by,
Again are all folk round the running place,
Nor other seems the dismal pageantry
Than heretofore, but that another face
Looks o'er the smooth course ready for the race,
For now, beheld of all, Milanion
Stands on the spot he twice has looked upon.

But yet—what change is this that holds the maid?
Does she indeed see in his glittering eye
More than disdain of the sharp shearing blade,
Some happy hope of help and victory?
The others seemed to say, "We come to die,
Look down upon us for a little while,
That dead, we may bethink us of thy smile."

But he—what look of mastery was this
He cast on her? why were his lips so red?
Why was his face so flushed with happiness?
So looks not one who deems himself but dead,
E'en if to death he bows a willing head;
So rather looks a god well pleased to find
Some earthly damsel fashioned to his mind.

Why must she drop her lids before his gaze,
And even as she casts adown her eyes
Redden to note his eager glance of praise,
And wish that she were clad in other guise?
Why must the memory to her heart arise
Of things unnoticed when they first were heard,
Some lover's song, some answering maiden's word?

What makes these longings, vague, without a name,
And this vain pity never felt before,
This sudden languor, this contempt of fame,
This tender sorrow for the time past o'er,
These doubts that grow each minute more and more?
Why does she tremble as the time grows near,
And weak defeat and woeful victory fear?

Now while she seemed to hear her beating heart,
Above their heads the trumpet blast rang out
And forth they sprang; and she must play her part.
Then flew her white feet, knowing not a doubt,

Though slackening once, she turned her head about,
But then she cried aloud and faster fled
Than e'er before, and all men deemed him dead.

But with no sound he raised aloft his hand,
And thence what seemed a ray of light there flew
And past the maid rolled on along the sand;
Then trembling she her feet together drew
And in her heart a strong desire there grew
To have the toy; some god she thought had given
That gift to her, to make of earth a heaven.

Then from the course with eager steps she ran,
And in her odorous bosom laid the gold.
But when she turned again, the great-limbed man
Now well ahead she failed not to behold,
And mindful of her glory waxing cold,
Sprang up and followed him in hot pursuit,
Though with one hand she touched the golden fruit.

Note too, the bow that she was wont to bear
She laid aside to grasp the glittering prize,
And o'er her shoulder from the quiver fair
Three arrows fell and lay before her eyes
Unnoticed, as amidst the people's cries
She sprang to head the strong Milanion,
Who now the turning-post had well-nigh won.

But as he set his mighty hand on it
White fingers underneath his own were laid,
And white limbs from his dazzled eyes did flit,
Then he the second fruit cast by the maid,
But she ran on awhile, then as one afraid
Wavered and stopped, and turned and made no stay,
Until the globe with its bright fellow lay.

Then, as a troubled glance she cast around
Now far ahead the Argive could she see,
And in her garment's hem one hand she wound

To keep the double prize, and strenuously
Sped o'er the course, and little doubt had she
To win the day, though now but scanty space
Was left betwixt him and the winning place.

Short was the way unto such winged feet,
Quickly she gained upon him till at last
He turned about her eager eyes to meet
And from his hand the third fair apple cast.
She wavered not, but turned and ran so fast
After the prize that should her bliss fulfil,
That in her hand it lay ere it was still.

Nor did she rest, but turned about to win
Once more, an unblest woeful victory—
And yet—and yet—why does her breath begin
To fail her, and her feet drag heavily?
Why fails she now to see if far or nigh
The goal is? why do her gray eyes grow dim?
Why do these tremors run through every limb?

She spreads her arms abroad some stay to find
Else must she fall, indeed, and findeth this,
A strong man's arms about her body twined,
Nor may she shudder now to feel his kiss,
So wrapped she is in new unbroken bliss:
Made happy that the foe the prize hath won.
She weeps glad tears for all her glory done.

Shatter the trumpet, hew adown the posts!
Upon the brazen altar break the sword,
And scatter incense to appease the ghosts
Of those who died here by their own award.
Bring forth the image of the mighty Lord,
And her who unseen o'er the runners hung,
And did a deed for ever to be sung.

Here are the gathered folk, make no delay,
Open King Schoeneus' well-filled treasury,
Bring out the gifts long hid from light of day,
The golden bowls o'erwrought with imagery,
Gold chains, and unguents brought from over sea,
The saffron gown the old Phoenician brought,
Within the temple of the Goddess wrought.

O ye, O damsels, who shall never see
Her, that Love's servant bringeth now to you,
Returning from another victory,
In some cool bower do all that now is due!
Since she in token of her service new
Shall give to Venus offerings rich enow,
Her maiden zone, her arrows, and her bow.

THE SACRILEGE

A Ballad-Tragedy (Circa 182–)

Part I

"I have a Love I love too well
Where Dunkery frowns on Exon Moor;
I have a Love I love too well,
        To whom, ere she was mine,
'Such is my love for you,' I said,
'That you shall have to hood your head
A silken kerchief crimson-red
        Wove finest of the fine.'

"And since this Love, for one mad moon,
On Exon Wild by Dunkery Tor,
Since this my Love for one mad moon
        Did clasp me as her king,
I snatched a silk-piece red and rare
From off a stall at Priddy Fair,
For handkerchief to hood her hair
        When we went gallanting.

"Full soon the four weeks neared their end
Where Dunkery frowns on Exon Moor;
And when the four weeks neared their end,
    And their swift sweets outwore,
I said, 'What shall I do to own
Those beauties bright as tulips blown,
And keep you here with me alone
    As mine for evermore?'

"And as she drowsed within my van
On Exon Wild by Dunkery Tor—
And as she drowsed within my van,
    And dawning turned to day,
She heavily raised her sloe-black eyes
And murmured back in softest wise,
'One more thing, and the charms you prize
    Are yours henceforth for aye.

'And swear I will I'll never go
While Dunkery frowns on Exon Moor
To meet the Cornish Wrestler Joe
    For dance and dallyings;
If you'll to yon cathedral shrine,
And finger from the chest divine
Treasure to buy me ear-drops fine,
    And richly jeweled rings.'

"I said: 'I am one who has gathered gear
From Marlbury Downs to Dunkery Tor,
Who has gathered gear for many a year
    From mansion, mart and fair;
But at God's house I've stayed my hand,
Hearing within me some command—
Curbed by a law not of the land
    From doing damage there!'

"Whereat she pouts, this Love of mine,
As Dunkery pouts to Exon Moor,

And still she pouts, this Love of mine,
So cityward I go.
But ere I start to do the thing,
And speed my soul's imperiling
For one who is my ravishing
And all the joy I know,

"I come to lay this charge on thee—
On Exon Wild by Dunkery Tor—
I come to lay this charge on thee
With solemn speech and sign:
Should things go ill, and my life pay
For botchery in this rash assay,
You are to take hers likewise—yea,
The month the law takes mine.

"For should my rival, Wrestler Joe,
Where Dunkery frowns on Exon Moor—
My reckless rival, Wrestler Joe,
My Love's bedwinner be,
My rafted spirit would not rest,
But wander weary and distrest
Throughout the world in wild protest:
The thought nigh maddens me!"

PART II

Thus did he speak—this brother of mine—
On Exon Wild by Dunkery Tor,
Born at my birth of mother of mine,
And forthwith went his way
To dare the deed some coming night . . .
I kept the watch with shaking sight,
The moon at moments breaking bright,
At others glooming gray.

The Sacrilege

For three full days I heard no sound
Where Dunkery frowns on Exon Moor,
I heard no sound at all around
    Whether his fay prevailed,
Or one more foul the master were,
Till some afoot did tidings bear
How that, for all his practiced care,
    He had been caught and jailed.

They had heard a crash when twelve had chimed
By Mendip east of Dunkery Tor,
When twelve had chimed and moonlight climbed;
    They watched, and he was tracked
By arch and aisle and saint and knight
Of sculptured stonework sheeted white
In the cathedral's ghostly light,
    And captured in the act.

Yes; for this Love he loved too well
Where Dunkery sights the Severn shore,
All for this Love he loved too well
    He burst the holy bars,
Seized golden vessels from the chest
To buy her ornaments of the best,
At her ill-witchery's request
    And lure of eyes like stars . . .

When blustering March confused the sky
In Toneborough Town by Exon Moor,
When blustering March confused the sky
    They stretched him; and he died.
Down in the crowd where I, to see
The end of him, stood silently,
With a set face he lipped to me—
    "Remember." "Ay!" I cried.

By night and day I shadowed her
From Toneborough Deane to Dunkery Tor,

I shadowed her asleep, astir,
        And yet I could not bear—
Till Wrestler Joe anon began
To figure as her chosen man,
And took her to his shining van—
        To doom a form so fair!

He made it handsome for her sake—
And Dunkery smiled to Exon Moor—
He made it handsome for his sake,
        Painting it out and in;
And on the door of apple-green
A bright brass knocker soon was seen,
And window-curtains white and clean
        For her to sit within.

And all could see she clave to him
As cleaves a cloud to Dunkery Tor,
Yea, all could see she clave to him,
        And every day I said,
"A pity it seems to part those two
That hourly grow to love more true:
Yet she's the wanton woman who
        Sent one to swing till dead!"

That blew to blazing all my hate,
While Dunkery frowned on Exon Moor,
And when the river swelled, her fate
        Came to her pitilessly . . .
I dogged her, crying: "Across that plank
They use as bridge to reach yon bank
A coat and hat lie limp and dank;
        Your goodman's, can they be?"

She paled, and went, I close behind—
And Exon frowned to Dunkery Tor,
She went, and I came up behind
        And tipped the plank that bore

Her, fleetly flitting across to eye
What such might bode. She slid awry:
And from the current came a cry,
A gurgle; and no more.

How that befell no mortal knew
From Marlbury Downs to Exon Moor;
No mortal knew that deed undue
But he who schemed the crime,
Which night still covers . . . But in dream
Those ropes of hair upon the stream
He sees, and he will hear that scream
Until his judgment-time.

Oscar Wilde

THE BALLAD OF READING GAOL

I

He did not wear his scarlet coat,
    For blood and wine are red,
And blood and wine were on his hands
    When they found him with the dead,
The poor dead woman whom he loved,
    And murdered in her bed.

He walked amongst the Trial Men
    In a suit of shabby gray;
A cricket cap was on his head,
    And his step seemed light and gay;
But I never saw a man who looked
    So wistfully at the day.

I never saw a man who looked
    With such a wistful eye
Upon that little tent of blue
    Which prisoners call the sky,
And at every drifting cloud that went
    With sails of silver by.

I walked, with other souls in pain,
Within another ring,
And was wondering if the man had done
A great or little thing.
When a voice behind me whispered low,
"*That fellow's got to swing.*"

Dear Christ! the very prison walls
Suddenly seemed to reel,
And the sky above my head became
Like a casque of scorching steel;
And, though I was a soul in pain,
My pain I could not feel.

I only knew what hunted thought
Quickened his step, and why
He looked upon the garish day
With such a wistful eye;
The man had killed the thing he loved,
And so he had to die.

Yet each man kills the thing he loves,
By each let this be heard,
Some do it with a bitter look,
Some with a flattering word,
The coward does it with a kiss,
The brave man with a sword!

Some kill their love when they are young,
And some when they are old;
Some strangle with the hands of Lust,
Some with the hands of Gold:
The kindest use a knife, because
The dead so soon grow cold.

Some love too little, some too long,
Some sell, and others buy;
Some do the deed with many tears,

And some without a sigh:
For each man kills the thing he loves,
Yet each man does not die.

He does not die a death of shame
On a day of dark disgrace,
Nor have a noose about his neck,
Nor a cloth upon his face,
Nor drop feet foremost through the floor
Into an empty space.

He does not sit with silent men
Who watch him night and day;
Who watch him when he tries to weep,
And when he tries to pray;
Who watch him lest himself should rob
The prison of its prey.

He does not wake at dawn to see
Dread figures throng his room,
The shivering Chaplain robed in white,
The Sheriff stern with gloom,
And the Governor all in shiny black,
With the yellow face of Doom.

He does not rise in piteous haste
To put on convict-clothes,
While some coarse-mouthed Doctor gloats, and notes
Each new and nerve-twitched pose,
Fingering a watch whose little ticks
Are like horrible hammer-blows.

He does not know that sickening thirst
That sands one's throat, before
The hangman with his gardener's gloves
Slips through the padded door,
And binds one with three leathern thongs,
That the throat may thirst no more.

He does not bend his head to hear
The Burial Office read,
Nor while the terror of his soul
Tells him he is not dead,
Cross his own coffin, as he moves
Into the hideous shed.

He does not stare upon the air
Through a little roof of glass:
He does not pray with lips of clay
For his agony to pass;
Nor feel upon his shuddering cheek
The kiss of Caiaphas.

II

Six weeks our guardsman walked the yard,
In the suit of shabby gray:
His cricket cap was on his head,
And his step seemed light and gay,
But I never saw a man who looked
So wistfully at the day.

I never saw a man who looked
With such a wistful eye
Upon that little tent of blue
Which prisoners call the sky,
And at every wandering cloud that trailed
Its raveled fleeces by.

He did not wring his hands, as do
Those witless men who dare
To try to rear the changeling Hope
In the cave of black Despair:
He only looked upon the sun,
And drank the morning air.

He did not wring his hands nor weep,
Nor did he peek or pine,

But he drank the air as though it held
Some healthful anodyne;
With open mouth he drank the sun
As though it had been wine!

And I and all the souls in pain,
Who tramped the other ring,
Forgot if we ourselves had done
A great or little thing,
And watched with gaze of dull amaze
The man who had to swing.

And strange it was to see him pass
With a step so light and gay,
And strange it was to see him look
So wistfully at the day,
And strange it was to think that he
Had such a debt to pay.

For oak and elm have pleasant leaves
That in the spring-time shoot:
But grim to see is the gallows-tree,
With its adder-bitten root,
And, green or dry, a man must die
Before it bears its fruit!

The loftiest place is that seat of grace
For which all worldlings try:
But who would stand in hempen band
Upon a scaffold high,
And through a murderer's collar take
His last look at the sky?

It is sweet to dance to violins
When Love and Life are fair;
To dance to flutes, to dance to lutes
Is delicate and rare:
But it is not sweet with nimble feet
To dance upon the air!

So with curious eyes and sick surmise
We watched him day by day,
And wondered if each one of us
Would end the self-same way,
For none can tell to what red Hell
His sightless soul may stray.

At last the dead man walked no more
Amongst the Trial Men,
And I knew that he was standing up
In the black dock's dreadful pen,
And that never would I see his face
In God's sweet world again.

Like two doomed ships that pass in storm
We had crossed each other's way:
But we made no sign, we said no word,
We had no word to say;
For we did not meet in the holy night,
But in the shameful day.

A prison wall was round us both,
Two outcast men we were:
The world had thrust us from its heart,
And God from out His care:
And the iron gin that waits for Sin
Had caught us in its snare.

III

In Debtors' Yard the stones are hard,
And the dripping wall is high,
So it was there he took the air
Beneath the leaden sky,
And by each side a Warder walked,
For fear the man might die.

Or else he sat with those who watched
His anguish night and day;
Who watched him when he rose to weep,
And when he crouched to pray;
Who watched him lest himself should rob
Their scaffold of its prey.

The Governor was strong upon
The Regulations Act:
The Doctor said that Death was but
A scientific fact:
And twice a day the Chaplain called,
And left a little tract.

And twice a day he smoked his pipe,
And drank his quart of beer:
His soul was resolute, and held
No hiding-place for fear;
He often said that he was glad
The hangman's hands were near.

But why he said so strange a thing
No Warder dared to ask:
For he to whom a watcher's doom
Is given as his task,
Must set a lock upon his lips,
And make his face a mask.

Or else he might be moved, and try
To comfort or console;

And what should Human Pity do
  Pent up in Murderer's Hole?
What word of grace in such a place
  Could help a brother's soul?

With slouch and swing around the ring
  We trod the Fools' Parade!
We did not care: we knew we were
  The Devil's Own Brigade:
And shaven head and feet of lead
  Make a merry masquerade.

We tore the tarry rope to shreds
  With blunt and bleeding nails;
We rubbed the doors, and scrubbed the floors,
  And cleaned the shining rails:
And, rank by rank, we soaped the plank,
  And clattered with the pails.

We sewed the sacks, we broke the stones,
  We turned the dusty drill:
We banged the tins, and bawled the hymns,
  And sweated on the mill:
But in the heart of every man
  Terror was lying still.

So still it lay that every day
  Crawled like a weed-clogged wave:
And we forgot the bitter lot
  That waits for fool and knave,
Till once, as we tramped in from work,
  We passed an open grave.

With yawning mouth the yellow hole
  Gaped for a living thing;
The very mud cried out for blood
  To the thirsty asphalt ring:
And we knew that ere one dawn grew fair
  Some prisoner had to swing.

Right in we went, with soul intent
On Death and Dread and Doom:
The hangman, with his little bag,
Went shuffling through the gloom:
And each man trembled as he crept
Into his numbered tomb.

That night the empty corridors
Were full of forms of Fear,
And up and down the iron town
Stole feet we could not hear,
And through the bars that hide the stars
White faces seemed to peer.

He lay as one who lies and dreams
In a pleasant meadow-land,
The watchers watched him as he slept,
And could not understand
How one could sleep so sweet a sleep
With a hangman close at hand.

But there is no sleep when men must weep
Who never yet have wept:
So we—the fool, the fraud, the knave—
That endless vigil kept,
And through each brain on hands of pain
Another's terror crept.

Alas! it is a fearful thing
To feel another's guilt!
For, right within, the sword of Sin
Pierced to its poisoned hilt,
And as molten lead were the tears we shed
For the blood we had not spilt.

The Warders with their shoes of felt
Crept by each padlocked door,
And peeped and saw, with eyes of awe,
Gray figures on the floor,

And wondered why men knelt to pray
Who never prayed before.

All through the night we knelt and prayed,
Mad mourners of a corse!
The troubled plumes of midnight were
The plumes upon a hearse:
And bitter wine upon a sponge
Was the savor of Remorse.

The gray cock crew, the red cock crew,
But never came the day:
And crooked shapes of Terror crouched,
In the corners where we lay:
And each evil sprite that walks by night
Before us seemed to play.

They glided past, they glided fast,
Like travelers through a mist:
They mocked the moon in a rigadoon
Of delicate turn and twist,
And with formal pace and loathsome grace
The phantoms kept their tryst.

With mop and mow, we saw them go,
Slim shadows hand in hand:
About, about, in ghostly rout
They trod a saraband:
And the damned grotesques made arabesques,
Like the wind upon the sand!

With the pirouettes of marionettes,
They tripped on pointed tread:
But with flutes of Fear they filled the ear,
As their grisly masque they led,
And loud they sang, and long they sang,
For they sang to wake the dead.

"*Oho!*" they cried, "*The world is wide,*
But fettered limbs go lame!
And once, or twice, to throw the dice
Is a gentlemanly game,
But he does not win who plays with Sin
In the secret House of Shame."

No things of air these antics were,
That frolicked with such glee:
To men whose lives were held in gyves
And whose feet might not go free,
Ah! wounds of Christ! they were living things,
Most terrible to see.

Around, around, they waltzed and wound;
Some wheeled in smirking pairs;
With the mincing step of a demirep
Some sidled up the stairs:
And with subtle sneer, and fawning leer,
Each helped us at our prayers.

The morning wind began to moan,
But still the night went on:
Through its giant loom the web of gloom
Crept till each thread was spun:
And, as we prayed, we grew afraid
Of the Justice of the Sun.

The moaning wind went wandering round
The weeping prison-wall:
Till like a wheel of turning steel
We felt the minutes crawl:
O moaning wind! what had we done
To have such a seneschal?

At last I saw the shadowed bars,
Like a lattice wrought in lead,
Move right across the whitewashed wall
That faced my three-plank bed,
And I knew that somewhere in the world
God's dreadful dawn was red.

At six o'clock we cleaned our cells,
At seven all was still,
But the sough and swing of a mighty wing
The prison seemed to fill,
For the Lord of Death with icy breath
Had entered in to kill.

He did not pass in purple pomp,
Nor ride a moon-white steed.
Three yards of cord and a sliding board
Are all the gallows' need:
So with rope of shame the Herald came
To do the secret deed.

We were as men who through a fen
Of filthy darkness grope:
We did not dare to breathe a prayer,
Or to give our anguish scope:
Something was dead in each of us,
And what was dead was Hope.

For Man's grim Justice goes its way,
And will not swerve aside:
It slays the weak, it slays the strong,

It has a deadly stride:
With iron heel it slays the strong,
The monstrous parricide!

We waited for the stroke of eight:
Each tongue was thick with thirst:
For the stroke of eight is the stroke of Fate
That makes a man accursed,
And Fate will use a running noose
For the best man and the worst.

We had no other thing to do,
Save to wait for the sign to come:
So, like things of stone in a valley lone,
Quiet we sat and dumb:
But each man's heart beat thick and quick,
Like a madman on a drum!

With sudden shock the prison-clock
Smote on the shivering air,
And from all the gaol rose up a wail
Of impotent despair,
Like the sound that frightened marshes hear
From some leper in his lair.

And as one sees most fearful things
In the crystal of a dream,
We saw the greasy hempen rope
Hooked to the blackened beam,
And heard the prayer the hangman's snare
Strangled into a scream.

And all the woe that moved him so
That he gave that bitter cry,
And the wild regrets, and the bloody sweats,
None knew so well as I:
For he who lives more lives than one
More deaths than one must die.

IV

There is no chapel on the day
    On which they hang a man:
The Chaplain's heart is far too sick,
    Or his face is far too wan,
Or there is that written in his eyes
    Which none should look upon.

So they kept us close till nigh on noon,
    And then they rang the bell,
And the Warders with their jingling keys
    Opened each listening cell,
And down the iron stair we tramped,
    Each from his separate Hell.

Out into God's sweet air we went,
    But not in wonted way,
For this man's face was white with fear,
    And that man's face was gray,
And I never saw sad men who looked
    So wistfully at the day.

I never saw sad men who looked
    With such a wistful eye
Upon that little tent of blue
    We prisoners called the sky,
And at every careless cloud that passed
    In happy freedom by.

But there were those amongst us all
    Who walked with downcast head,
And knew that, had each got his due,
    They should have died instead:
He had but killed a thing that lived,
    Whilst they had killed the dead.

For he who sins a second time
    Wakes a dead soul to pain,

And draws it from its spotted shroud,
    And makes it bleed again,
And makes it bleed great gouts of blood,
    And makes it bleed in vain!

Like ape or clown, in monstrous garb
    With crooked arrows starred,
Silently we went round and round
    The slippery asphalt yard;
Silently we went round and round,
    And no man spoke a word.

Silently we went round and round
    And through each hollow mind
The Memory of dreadful things
    Rushed like a dreadful wind,
And Horror stalked before each man,
    And Terror crept behind.

The Warders strutted up and down,
    And kept their herd of brutes,
Their uniforms were spick and span,
    And they wore their Sunday suits,
But we knew the work they had been at,
    By the quicklime on their boots.

For where a grave had opened wide,
    There was no grave at all:
Only a stretch of mud and sand
    By the hideous prison-wall,
And a little heap of burning lime,
    That the man should have his pall.

For he has a pall, this wretched man,
    Such as few men can claim:
Deep down below a prison-yard,
    Naked for greater shame,
He lies, with fetters on each foot,
    Wrapt in a sheet of flame!

And all the while the burning lime
 Eats flesh and bone away,
It eats the brittle bone by night,
 And the soft flesh by day,
It eats the flesh and bone by turns,
 But it eats the heart alway.

For three long years they will not sow
 Or root or seedling there:
For three long years the unbless'd spot
 Will sterile be and bare,
And look upon the wondering sky
 With unreproachful stare.

They think a murderer's heart would taint
 Each simple seed they sow.
It is not true! God's kindly earth
 Is kindlier than men know,
And the red rose would but blow more red,
 The white rose whiter blow.

Out of his mouth a red, red rose!
 Out of his heart a white!
For who can say by what strange way,
 Christ brings His will to light,
Since the barren staff the pilgrim bore
 Bloomed in the great Pope's sight?

But neither milk-white rose nor red
 May bloom in prison-air;
The shard, the pebble, and the flint,
 Are what they give us there:
For flowers have been known to heal
 A common man's despair.

So never will wine-red rose or white,
 Petal by petal, fall
On that stretch of mud and sand that lies

By the hideous prison-wall,
To tell the men who tramp the yard
That God's Son died for all.

Yet though the hideous prison-wall
Still hems him round and round,
And a spirit may not walk by night
That is with fetters bound,
And a spirit may but weep that lies
In such unholy ground,

He is at peace—this wretched man—
At peace, or will be soon:
There is no thing to make him mad,
Nor does Terror walk at noon,
For the lampless Earth in which he lies
Has neither Sun nor Moon.

They hanged him as a beast is hanged:
They did not even toll
A requiem that might have brought
Rest to his startled soul,
But hurriedly they took him out.
And hid him in a hole.

They stripped him of his canvas clothes,
And gave him to the flies:
They mocked the swollen purple throat,
And the stark and staring eyes:

And with laughter loud they heaped the shroud
In which their convict lies.

The Chaplain would not kneel to pray
By his dishonored grave:
Nor mark it with that blessed Cross
That Christ for sinners gave,
Because the man was one of those
Whom Christ came down to save.

Yet all is well; he has but passed
To Life's appointed bourne:
And alien tears will fill for him
Pity's long-broken urn,
For his mourners will be outcast men,
And outcasts always mourn.

V

I know not whether Laws be right,
Or whether Laws be wrong;
All that we know who lie in gaol
Is that the wall is strong;
And that each day is like a year,
A year whose days are long.

But this I know, that every Law
That men have made for Man,
Since first Man took his brother's life,
And the sad world began,
But straws the wheat and saves the chaff
With a most evil fan.

This too I know—and wise it were
If each could know the same—
That every prison that men build
Is built with bricks of shame,
And bound with bars lest Christ should see
How men their brothers maim.

With bars they blur the gracious moon,
And blind the goodly sun:
And they do well to hide their Hell,
For in it things are done
That Son of God nor son of Man
Ever should look upon!

The vilest deeds like poison weeds
Bloom well in prison-air:
It is only what is good in Man
That wastes and withers there:
Pale Anguish keeps the heavy gate,
And the Warder is Despair.

For they starve the little frightened child
Till it weeps both night and day:
And they scourge the weak, and flog the fool,
And gibe the old and gray,
And some grow mad, and all grow bad,
And none a word may say.

Each narrow cell in which we dwell
Is a foul and dark latrine,
And the fetid breath of living Death
Chokes up each grated screen,
And all, but Lust, is turned to dust
In Humanity's machine.

The brackish water that we drink
Creeps with a loathsome slime,
And the bitter bread they weigh in scales
Is full of chalk and lime,
And Sleep will not lie down, but walks
Wild-eyed, and cries to Time.

But though lean Hunger and green Thirst
Like asp with adder fight,
We have little care of prison fare,

For what chills and kills outright
Is that every stone one lifts by day
Becomes one's heart by night.

With midnight always in one's heart,
And twilight in one's cell,
We turn the crank, or tear the rope,
Each in his separate Hell,
And the silence is more awful far
Than the sound of a brazen bell.

And never a human voice comes near
To speak a gentle word:
And the eye that watches through the door
Is pitiless and hard:
And by all forgot, we rot and rot,
With soul and body marred.

And thus we rust Life's iron chain
Degraded and alone:
And some men curse, and some men weep,
And some men make no moan:
But God's eternal Laws are kind
And break the heart of stone.

And every human heart that breaks,
In prison-cell or yard,
Is as that broken box that gave
Its treasure to the Lord,
And filled the unclean leper's house
With the scent of costliest nard.

Ah! happy they whose hearts can break
And peace of pardon win!
How else may man make straight his plan
And cleanse his soul from Sin?
How else but through a broken heart
May Lord Christ enter in?

And he of the swollen purple throat,
    And the stark and staring eyes,
Waits for the holy hands that took
    The Thief to Paradise;
And a broken and a contrite heart
    The Lord will not despise.

The man in red who reads the Law
    Gave him three weeks of life,
Three little weeks in which to heal
    His soul of his soul's strife,
And cleanse from every blot of blood
    The hand that held the knife.

And with tears of blood he cleansed the hand,
    The hand that held the steel:
For only blood can wipe out blood,
    And only tears can heal:
And the crimson stain that was of Cain
    Became Christ's snow-white seal.

VI

In Reading gaol by Reading town
    There is a pit of shame,
And in it lies a wretched man
    Eaten by teeth of flame,
In a burning winding-sheet he lies,
    And his grave has got no name.

And there, till Christ call forth the dead,
In silence let him lie:
No need to waste the foolish tear,
Or heave the windy sigh:
The man had killed the thing he loved,
And so he had to die.

And all men kill the thing they love,
By all let this be heard,
Some do it with a bitter look,
Some with a flattering word,
The coward does it with a kiss,
The brave man with a sword!

AN AUTHOR'S NOTES

Poems in the form of stories and narratives make up a large part of the works of the nineteenth century English poets, and indeed many of them are long enough to be whole books in themselves.

Some of these poems are directed at social ills or situations of the day; some are drawn from legend and epic, or from history; yet others are more purely romantic or imaginary. Often they have strong elements of gloom and foreboding and remoteness. One of the poems in this selection is drawn from direct personal experience—"The Ballad of Reading Gaol."

The Prisoner of Chillon

The Château de Chillon still stands; it juts into the northern side of Lake Geneva (Lake Leman). Byron's prisoner is François de Bonnivard (*c.* 1493–1570), a prior who supported Geneva's revolt against Charles III of Savoy and was twice imprisoned by him in the castle.

Arethusa

This is from the classical story. Arethusa was a water nymph who was turned into a fountain while Alpheus was pursuing her—but he caught her just the same.

The Eve of St. Agnes

St. Agnes is the patron saint of girls. A fourth century Roman virgin of noble birth, she was martyred at the age of thirteen for rejecting a pagan suitor. Her feast day is January 21st—always a chilly time of the year. The poem refers to a superstition connected with her day.

Lady Geraldine's Courtship

This gives a feeling of social distinctions that existed in England until well into the twentieth century. Robert Browning admired the poem and so wrote to the semi-invalid poetess, Miss Elizabeth Barrett—which began their long and romantic association. She wasn't so keen on the work herself as she wrote most of it in a hurry to satisfy her publisher.

Morte d'Arthur

This was written in 1835, but Tennyson later incorporated it in his long epic, "The Idylls of the King," which was published in 1859.

The Revenge

The battle took place in 1591. Sir Thomas Howard's fleet was out to capture the Spanish treasure ships on their way home—a kind of licensed piracy. Finding the odds against him he withdrew; but the *Revenge* became separated from the rest of the fleet and Sir Richard Grenville, hopelessly outnumbered, fought fifteen ships as he tried to break through the Spanish line.

"Childe Roland to the Dark Tower Came"

The prefix "Childe" means a youth of noble birth who has yet to prove his knighthood. The title—and last line—of the poem is taken from a line in Shakespeare's *King Lear*.

On being questioned about the poem, Browning acknowledged that the central purpose was constancy to an ideal—"He that endureth to the end shall be saved."

Sohrab and Rustum

Matthew Arnold based this story on an episode from "Shãhnãma" by the great tenth century Persian poet, Firdusi.

Atalanta's Race

This is a combination of several versions of the classical story. It is the first of the twenty-four tales in *The Earthly Paradise*, which are drawn from various folk and classical sources. Like most of Morris' works it was published by his own Kelmscott Press, with his own Pre-Raphaelite designs.

The Ballad of Reading Gaol

This was dedicated: "*In Memoriam C.T.W.: Sometime Trooper of the Royal Horse Guards. Obiit H.M.Prison, Reading Berkshire, July 7th, 1896.*" "C.T.W." was Charles T. Wooldridge, who was executed for the murder of his wife while Oscar Wilde was also imprisoned in Reading. The poem contains a strong plea against capital punishment.